KING
LOUIS XIV

D1609095

KING
LOUIS XIV

Pierre L. Horn

1986
CHELSEA HOUSE PUBLISHERS
NEW YORK
NEW HAVEN   PHILADELPHIA

SENIOR EDITOR: William P. Hansen
PROJECT EDITOR: John W. Selfridge
ASSOCIATE EDITOR: Marian W. Taylor
EDITORIAL COORDINATOR: Karyn Gullen Browne
EDITORIAL STAFF: Maria Behan
　　　　　　　　Pierre Hauser
　　　　　　　　Perry Scott King
　　　　　　　　Kathleen McDermott
　　　　　　　　Howard Ratner
　　　　　　　　Alma Rodriguez-Sokol
　　　　　　　　Bert Yaeger
ART DIRECTOR: Susan Lusk
LAYOUT: Irene Friedman
ART ASSISTANTS: Noreen Lamb
　　　　　　　　Victoria Tomaselli
COVER ILLUSTRATION: Michael Garland
PICTURE RESEARCH: Diane Wallis

First Printing

Library of Congress Cataloging in Publication Data

Horn, Pierre. LOUIS XIV.

(World leaders past & present)
Bibliography: p.
Includes index.

1. Louis XIV, King of France, 1638–1715—Juvenile literature.
2. France—King and ruler—Biography—Juvenile literature.
3. France—History—Louis XIV, 1643–1715—Juvenile literature.
[1. Louis XIV, King of France, 1638–1715. 2. King, queens, rulers,
etc. 3. France—History—Louis XIV, 1643–1715] I. Title II. Series.
DC129.H67 1986　　　　　944'.033'0924　　　　[B] [92] 86-13659
ISBN 0-87754-591-X

Chelsea House Publishers
Harold Steinberg, Chairman and Publisher
Susan Lusk, Vice President
A Division of Chelsea House Educational Communications, Inc.

133 Christopher Street, New York, NY 10014

345 Whitney Avenue, New Haven, CT 06510

5014 West Chester Pike, Edgemont, PA 19028

Contents

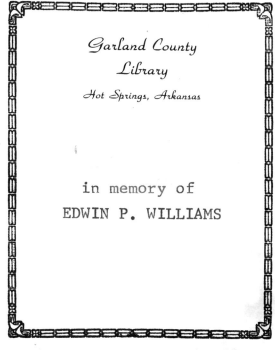

CHELSEA HOUSE PUBLISHERS

WORLD LEADERS PAST & PRESENT

ADENAUER
ALEXANDER THE GREAT
MARK ANTONY
KING ARTHUR
KEMAL ATATÜRK
CLEMENT ATTLEE
BEGIN
BEN-GURION
BISMARCK
LEON BLUM
BOLÍVAR
CESARE BORGIA
BRANDT
BREZHNEV
CAESAR
CALVIN
CASTRO
CATHERINE THE GREAT
CHARLEMAGNE
CHIANG KAI-SHEK
CHURCHILL
CLEMENCEAU
CLEOPATRA
CORTÉS
CROMWELL
DANTON
DE GAULLE
DE VALERA
DISRAELI
EISENHOWER
ELEANOR OF AQUITAINE
QUEEN ELIZABETH I
FERDINAND AND ISABELLA

FRANCO
FREDERICK THE GREAT
INDIRA GANDHI
GANDHI
GARIBALDI
GENGHIS KHAN
GLADSTONE
HAMMARSKJÖLD
HENRY VIII
HENRY OF NAVARRE
HINDENBURG
HITLER
HO CHI MINH
KING HUSSEIN
IVAN THE TERRIBLE
ANDREW JACKSON
JEFFERSON
JOAN OF ARC
POPE JOHN XXIII
LYNDON JOHNSON
BENITO JUÁREZ
JFK
KENYATTA
KHOMEINI
KHRUSHCHEV
MARTIN LUTHER KING, JR.
KISSINGER
LENIN
LINCOLN
LLOYD GEORGE
LOUIS XIV
LUTHER
JUDAS MACCABEUS
MAO

MARY, QUEEN OF SCOTS
GOLDA MEIR
METTERNICH
MUSSOLINI
NAPOLEON
NASSER
NEHRU
NERO
NICHOLAS II
NIXON
NKRUMAH
PERICLES
PERÓN
QADDAFI
ROBESPIERRE
ELEANOR ROOSEVELT
FDR
THEODORE ROOSEVELT
SADAT
STALIN
SUN YAT-SEN
TAMERLAINE
THATCHER
TITO
TROTSKY
TRUDEAU
TRUMAN
QUEEN VICTORIA
WASHINGTON
CHAIM WEIZMANN
WOODROW WILSON
XERXES
ZHOU ENLAI

ON LEADERSHIP

Arthur M. Schlesinger, jr.

LEADERSHIP, it may be said, is really what makes the world go round. Love no doubt smooths the passage; but love is a private transaction between consenting adults. Leadership is a public trans-action with history. The idea of leadership affirms the capacity of individuals to move, inspire and mobilize masses of people so that they act together in pursuit of an end. Sometimes leadership serves good purposes, sometimes bad; but whether the end is benign or evil, great leaders are those men and women who leave their personal stamp on history.

Now, the very concept of leadership implies the proposition that individuals can make a difference. This proposition has never been universally accepted. From classical times to the present day, eminent thinkers have regarded individuals as no more than the agents and pawns of larger forces, whether the gods and goddesses of the ancient world or, in the modern era, race, class, nation, the dialectic, the will of the people, the spirit of the times, history itself. Against such forces, the individual dwindles into insignificance.

So contends the thesis of historical determinism. Tolstoy's great novel *War and Peace* offers a famous statement of the case. Why, Tolstoy asked, did millions of men in the Napoleonic wars, denying their human feelings and their common sense, move back and forth across Europe slaughtering their fellows? "The war," Tolstoy answered, "was bound to happen simply because it was bound to happen." All prior history predetermined it. As for leaders, they, Tolstoy said, "are but the labels that serve to give a name to an end and, like labels, they have the least possible connection with the event." The greater the leader, "the more conspicuous the inevitability and the predestination of every act he commits." The leader, said Tolstoy, is "the slave of history."

Determinism takes many forms. Marxism is the determinism of class, Nazism the determinism of race. But the idea of men and women as the slaves of history runs athwart the deepest human instincts. Rigid determinism abolishes the idea of human freedom—the assumption of free choice that underlies every move we make, every word we speak, every thought we think. It abolishes the idea of human responsibility, since it is manifestly unfair to reward or punish people for actions that are by definition beyond their control. No one can live consistently by any deterministic creed. The Marxist states prove this themselves by their extreme susceptibility to the cult of leadership.

More than that, history refutes the idea that individuals make no difference. In December 1931 a British politician crossing Park Avenue in New York City between 76th and 77th Streets around ten-thirty at night looked in the wrong direction and was knocked down by an automobile—a moment, he later recalled, of a man aghast, a world aglare: "I do not understand why I was not broken like an eggshell or squashed like a gooseberry." Fourteen months later an American politician, sitting in an open car in Miami, Florida, was fired on by an assassin; the man beside him was hit. Those who believe that individuals make no difference to history might well ponder whether the next two decades would have been the same had Mario Contasini's car killed Winston Churchill in 1931 and Giuseppe Zangara's bullet killed Franklin Roosevelt in 1933. Suppose, in addition, that Adolf Hitler had been killed in the street fighting during the Munich *Putsch* of 1923 and that Lenin had died of typhus during the First World War. What would the 20th century be like now?

For better or for worse, individuals do make a difference. "The notion that a people can run itself and its affairs anonymously," wrote the philosopher William James, "is now well known to be the silliest of absurdities. Mankind does nothing save through initiatives on the part of inventors, great or small, and imitation by the rest of us—these are the sole factors in human progress. Individuals of genius show the way, and set the patterns, which common people then adopt and follow."

Leadership, James suggests, means leadership in thought as well as in action. In the long run, leaders in thought may well make the greater difference to the world. But, as Woodrow Wilson once said, "Those only are leaders of men, in the general eye, who lead in action. . . . It is at their hands that new thought gets its translation into the crude language of deeds." Leaders in thought often invent in solitude and obscurity, leaving to later generations the tasks of imitation. Leaders in action—the leaders portrayed in this series— have to be effective in their own time.

And they cannot be effective by themselves. They must act in response to the rhythms of their age. Their genius must be adapted, in a phrase of William James's, "to the receptivities of the moment." Leaders are useless without followers. "There goes the mob," said the French politician hearing a clamor in the streets. "I am their leader. I must follow them." Great leaders turn the inchoate emotions of the mob to purposes of their own. They seize on the opportunities of their time, the hopes, fears, frustrations, crises, potentialities.

They succeed when events have prepared the way for them, when the community is waiting to be aroused, when they can provide the clarifying and organizing ideas. Leadership ignites the circuit between the individual and the mass and thereby alters history.

It may alter history for better or for worse. Leaders have been responsible for the most extravagant follies and most monstrous crimes that have beset suffering humanity. They have also been vital in such gains as humanity has made in individual freedom, religious and racial tolerance, social justice and respect for human rights.

There is no sure way to tell in advance who is going to lead for good and who for evil. But a glance at the gallery of men and women in *World Leaders—Past and Present* suggests some useful tests.

One test is this: do leaders lead by force or by persuasion? By command or by consent? Through most of history leadership was exercised by the divine right of authority. The duty of followers was to defer and to obey. "Theirs not to reason why,/ Theirs but to do and die." On occasion, as with the so-called "enlightened despots" of the 18th century in Europe, absolutist leadership was animated by humane purposes. More often, absolutism nourished the passion for domination, land, gold and conquest and resulted in tyranny.

The great revolution of modern times has been the revolution of equality. The idea that all people should be equal in their legal condition has undermined the old structures of authority, hierarchy and deference. The revolution of equality has had two contrary effects on the nature of leadership. For equality, as Alexis de Tocqueville pointed out in his great study *Democracy in America*, might mean equality in servitude as well as equality in freedom.

"I know of only two methods of establishing equality in the political world," Tocqueville wrote. "Rights must be given to every citizen, or none at all to anyone . . . save one, who is the master of all." There was no middle ground "between the sovereignty of all and the absolute power of one man." In his astonishing prediction of 20th-century totalitarian dictatorship, Tocqueville explained how the revolution of equality could lead to the "*Führerprinzip*" and more terrible absolutism than the world had ever known.

But when rights are given to every citizen and the sovereignty of all is established, the problem of leadership takes a new form, becomes more exacting than ever before. It is easy to issue commands and enforce them by the rope and the stake, the concentration camp and the *gulag*. It is much harder to use argument and achievement to overcome opposition and win consent. The Founding Fathers of the United States understood the difficulty. They believed that history had given them the opportunity to decide, as

Alexander Hamilton wrote in the first Federalist Paper, whether men are indeed capable of basing government on "reflection and choice, or whether they are forever destined to depend . . . on accident and force."

Government by reflection and choice called for a new style of leadership and a new quality of followership. It required leaders to be responsive to popular concerns, and it required followers to be active and informed participants in the process. Democracy does not eliminate emotion from politics; sometimes it fosters demagoguery; but it is confident that, as the greatest of democratic leaders put it, you cannot fool all of the people all of the time. It measures leadership by results and retires those who overreach or falter or fail.

It is true that in the long run despots are measured by results too. But they can postpone the day of judgment, sometimes indefinitely, and in the meantime they can do infinite harm. It is also true that democracy is no guarantee of virtue and intelligence in government, for the voice of the people is not necessarily the voice of God. But democracy, by assuring the rights of opposition, offers built-in resistance to the evils inherent in absolutism. As the theologian Reinhold Niebuhr summed it up, "Man's capacity for justice makes democracy possible, but man's inclination to injustice makes democracy necessary."

A second test for leadership is the end for which power is sought. When leaders have as their goal the supremacy of a master race or the promotion of totalitarian revolution or the acquisition and exploitation of colonies or the protection of greed and privilege or the preservation of personal power, it is likely that their leadership will do little to advance the cause of humanity. When their goal is the abolition of slavery, the liberation of women, the enlargement of opportunity for the poor and powerless, the extension of equal rights to racial minorities, the defense of the freedoms of expression and opposition, it is likely that their leadership will increase the sum of human liberty and welfare.

Leaders have done great harm to the world. They have also conferred great benefits. You will find both sorts in this series. Even "good" leaders must be regarded with a certain wariness. Leaders are not demigods; they put on their trousers one leg after another just like ordinary mortals. No leader is infallible, and every leader needs to be reminded of this at regular intervals. Irreverence irritates leaders but is their salvation. Unquestioning submission corrupts leaders and demeans followers. Making a cult of a leader is always a mistake. Fortunately hero worship generates its own antidote. "Every hero," said Emerson, "becomes a bore at last."

The signal benefit the great leaders confer is to embolden the rest of us to live according to our own best selves, to be active, insistent, and resolute in affirming our own sense of things. For great leaders attest to the reality of human freedom against the supposed inevitabilities of history. And they attest to the wisdom and power that may lie within the most unlikely of us, which is why Abraham Lincoln remains the supreme example of great leadership. A great leader, said Emerson, exhibits new possibilities to all humanity. "We feed on genius. . . . Great men exist that there may be greater men."

Great leaders, in short, justify themselves by emancipating and empowering their followers. So humanity struggles to master its destiny, remembering with Alexis de Tocqueville: "It is true that around every man a fatal circle is traced beyond which he cannot pass; but within the wide verge of that circle he is powerful and free; as it is with man, so with communities."

—*New York*

1

A Turbulent Sky

Nicolas Fouquet cast a triumphant glance over the magnificent spectacle before him. Fouquet's newly completed residence, the château Vaux-le-Vicomte, now glittered with more than 6,000 celebrants. It was late summer, August 17, 1661, and the housewarming party was proving a success. From amid the opulent throng his eyes searched out the most prized guest of all: the 22-year-old king of France—Louis XIV. It was no longer satisfactory to be head of the king's treasury: Fouquet wanted to become the first minister, succeeding Cardinal Mazarin, who died earlier in the year. The king had only recently told his cabinet that no one would be appointed to the vacant post. But Fouquet remained unconcerned. He was certain that after tonight his vast show of wealth and hospitality would swiftly change the king's mind. He watched Louis toss back his head in laughter and move gracefully on through the crowd.

The château was reputed to be the most exquisite estate in the realm. Halfway between Paris and Fontainebleau, Fouquet's house was almost a palace, with its terraces and water works. Rumor held that the nearby river had been diverted to provide water

Louis's father, Louis XIII, whose stormy relationship with his wife was partly responsible for the coldness that he displayed toward his son. He was especially unhappy over his wife's decision to break with tradition by assuming personal responsibility for the boy's upbringing rather than having him looked after by servants.

Louis XIV (1638–1715) became nominal king of France upon the death of his father, Louis XIII (1601–43). Until he attained his legal majority in 1651, Louis was groomed for kingship by his mother, Anne of Austria (1601–66), who provided her son with a moral education as rigorous as the intellectual training he received from his tutors.

Following her husband's death, Anne of Austria assumed the regency of France, ruling on young Louis's behalf until 1651. During her regency, she entrusted all responsibility for affairs of state to her chief adviser and first minister, Italian-born diplomat and churchman Cardinal Jules Mazarin (1602–61).

for a thousand fountains, each streaming a torrent of water. The vast entourage was treated to music by the famous Jean-Baptiste Lully, a comedy by Molière, and such expensive gifts as diamond tiaras and saddle horses.

The young king of France did enjoy himself—perhaps more than he would have liked. Louis viewed the grand party and sumptuous château and all of the finery with envy. Fouquet's ostentation was inappropriate for a subject, especially one with responsibility for the king's finances. The superintendent even had the audacity to offer money and protection to one of Louis's mistresses—the passionate Louise de La Vallière. Fouquet had apparently been building his own realm within the king's. Louis knew he had to remove him.

The superintendent-general of finance was an influential figure and would be difficult to remove. In addition, Fouquet was the *procureur-général* (an important legal official) of the Paris Parlement, the lawmaking body of France. As such he could only be tried before Parlement. But Parlement was full of Fouquet's supporters. The king could not stalk him there—the base of his rival's strength.

In the weeks following the party, the king convinced Fouquet to sell his office on the grounds that such a position clashed with the complete devotion needed to serve the crown. Fouquet, never suspecting what Louis had in mind, complied with his king's wishes.

Louis made his move on September 5, 1661, his 23rd birthday. The king held court in Nantes, near Fouquet's fortress of Belle-Isle. After a meeting of the court, he left Fouquet with a smile to put off any suspicions. Louis tells the rest of the story in a letter to his mother dated September 15, 1661: "Madame, my Mother, I wrote to you this morning of the execution of my order for the arrest of the Superintendent; but I am now pleased to send you the details. You know that for some time I have had it in my heart, but it was impossible to do it earlier . . . You should have seen the difficulties I had in speaking to d'Artagnan [captain of the Musketeers], for I was burdened with a crowd of people, all of them alert, and they would have guessed my intention at the slightest inclination. . . . Nonetheless, two days ago I ordered him to be ready. . . .

"Finally this morning the Superintendent came to work with me as usual; I received him in one way or another, pretending to look for papers until I saw d'Artagnan through the window in the court . . . then I dismissed the Superintendent, who, after whispering a little with La Feuillade, disappeared . . . poor d'Artagnan thought that he had missed, and sent Maupertuis to me to say that he suspected that someone had warned him to flee. But he caught up with him in the square before the church and arrested him on my order at about noon.

"I have also ordered the companies of the guard . . . to maneuver . . . so that they would be ready to march on Belle-Isle . . . if by chance the Superintendent should make resistance there . . . I have talked about the incident with the gentlemen

> *The love of glory certainly takes precedence over all others in my soul.*
> —LOUIS XIV

around me . . . I told them frankly that I had formed the project four months ago . . . I told them that I would not have another superintendent . . . that I would work on the finances myself with the aid of the faithful people who would act under my direction, that this was the only true method of creating abundance [prosperity] and comfort for my people. You will have no trouble believing that these people are sheepish, but I am satisfied that they see that I am not so much a dupe as they thought, and that it would be wise to attach themselves to me. . . ."

A Chamber of Justice was created to try Fouquet. Unable to find him guilty of treason, they successfully prosecuted him for "careless" financial administration. The Chamber of Justice sentenced Fouquet to exile from France. Louis, however, overruled the court and condemned Fouquet to life imprisonment, which he served first in the Bastille, then in Pignerol Fortress, where he died in 1680. The concentration of power in the hands of the first minister with Mazarin, and Richelieu before him, had been swept aside. Louis XIV had established himself as the supreme ruler of France, which he regarded as his divine right. Louis would rule until his death by the famous political maxim attributed to him: *L'état, c'est moi* (I am the state). Setting himself at the luminous center of his nation, he would be known as the "Sun King."

Louis XIV, or Louis the Great, was the eldest son of King Louis XIII and Queen Anne of France. He was born on September 5, 1638, in the beautiful 16th-century castle of Saint-Germain-en-Laye, located in a small village west of Paris. The birth of a male baby to the royal family is usually the cause of nationwide celebration. The coming of Louis XIV was the cause of great joy throughout the country. At the time of his son's birth, King Louis XIII was ill and many feared that he would die without a legal heir. The baby boy was praised as a savior, "*Louis "le Dieudonné*"—Louis the Gift of God. Not everyone had cause to celebrate, however. The king's brother, Gaston of Orléans, was no longer next in line for the throne now that there was an heir apparent. Henry II, prince of Condé, an important province in the kingdom of France, though himself too old to ascend the throne, had two sons who were eligible. Gaston and Condé were not easily discouraged. To them, the birth of the dauphin (meaning the eldest son of the king of France and legal heir to the French monarchy) was a definite obstacle, but both men were powerful, influential, and quite capable of trying to remove it.

As was customary in other European royal families, it was assumed the boy would be taken from his parents and raised by servants. Queen Anne in no way wanted to give up her rights as mother. She decided personally to take responsibility for Louis's upbringing. One observer at court related that Anne "seldom leaves him, she takes great pleasure playing with him and wheeling him in his carriage in good weather. He is her principal pleasure, so much that there is no other in her heart." From the outset, Louis was showered with adoration. For most of his long life and 54-year reign, Louis was accustomed

Many French artists of the 17th century imitated the aesthetics of classical antiquity. Here a bust of the young Louis portrays him as an ancient Roman mythological deity. The wreath of laurel adorning his brow symbolizes victory.

to having unparalleled status among both his subjects and his courtiers.

Louis's closeness to his mother differed greatly from his relationship with his father. Coldness, rather than affection, prevailed between father and son. The stormy marriage of Louis XIII and Anne had probably done much to weaken the relationship between father and son. To his chief adviser and confidant, Cardinal Richelieu, the king once complained, "I am dissatisfied with my son . . . when he saw me he cried as if he had seen the devil, and ran to his mother."

A famous, though probably fictitious, story further illustrates Louis's feelings toward his father. The story describes a meeting between father and four-year-old son. Upon young Louis's return from his baptism, in 1642, the ailing king, propped up in bed, asked the boy his name. "Louis XIV," Louis replied. "Not yet, not yet!" cried the sad king.

The following year, on May 14, 1643, Louis XIII died of tuberculosis. The king and queen had taken precautions concerning his successor. In December 1642 Louis had registered a document in Parlement denying his brother Gaston any formal ties with the monarchy following Louis's death. Meanwhile, Anne pacified the prince of Condé, Henry II, by making to him various overtures and promises.

Louis was not even five years old when his father died. He would not achieve legal majority and thus the rule of France until age 13. Until then, his mother would act as regent while her chief minister, Cardinal Jules Mazarin, took care of the affairs of state.

An Italian scholar and papal diplomat, Mazarin entered French politics with the help of his mentor, Armand Jean du Plessis, Cardinal Richelieu, who persuaded the pope to appoint Mazarin a cardinal. On Richelieu's death in 1642, Mazarin was the obvious choice for the open position of chief minister of France. Mazarin took over Richelieu's role, quickly becoming involved in foreign policy.

At the time of Louis XIII's death, France was involved in the Thirty Years' War, which lasted from 1618 to 1648. Costly and seemingly endless, the

In one sense, Louis' childhood came to an end with the outbreak of the Frondes.
—RAGNHILD HATTON
British historian

conflict pitted the German Protestant princes, France, Sweden, Denmark, and England against the Catholic princes of Germany and the Holy Roman Empire, represented by the Hapsburg Empire of Austria, Spain, Bohemia, Italy, and Flanders. When Spanish troops attempted to invade France and reach Paris through her northern provinces, Louis II, the son of Henry II, defeated them at Rocroi on May 19, 1643. Spain's forces were decisively turned back at subsequent battles at Freiburg and Nordlingen. A final battle at Lens in August 1648 brought victory to the French army, led again by Louis II, now prince of Condé. Long-stymied treaty negotiations finally yielded peace to a ravaged Europe.

Through the Treaty of Westphalia in 1648, Mazarin was able to make Richelieu's vision of French territorial expansion a reality. German and Austrian power had been dealt substantial losses; in addition, France now possessed the province of Alsace and the three bishoprics of Toul, Metz, and Verdun in Lorraine on the German border. Mazarin's work on these treaties both concluded the war's devastion, and made France the leading power in Europe. Domestic conditions were another matter. While France was victorious abroad, poverty went unchecked at home.

On the political front, the monarchy was undergoing the threat of losing its rightful king. Louis had fallen ill. In November 1647 he contracted smallpox, a dreaded disease which was usually fatal. Paris began toasting Louis's uncle as King Gaston I. Louis's constitution was strong, however. He survived the symptoms of the disease, as well as the incisions of the lancets—small two-edged surgical knives used by surgeons for bloodletting (a technique used as recently as the 18th century). When the little king eventually recovered public rejoicing and celebration swept over France. Festivities were to prove short-lived, however. Economic collapse—the combined result of the war's attrition, bad harvest, and taxation—was generating unrest. Frustration over these conditions led many to turn against the state. Hunger was rampant.

In 1642, following a distinguished career as a papal diplomat, Mazarin became first minister of France. An able administrator with a deep understanding of foreign and domestic affairs, he provided Louis with a comprehensive education in statesmanship.

The plight of the common people was largely due to an unproductive, often cruel, economic system that had outlived its usefulness long ago.

Land, even rich acreage, was badly irrigated and drained; fertilization was also a problem since there were too few animals for manure; soil preparation was done with the help of a horse- or ox-drawn plow which made only shallow furrows; harrowing, or loosening the soil, was done with thorny bundles and did little against weeds and other harmful plants. Planting or sowing was primitive as well: peasants with folded aprons full of seeds would throw them into the wind, hoping they would land in the furrows. In the fall, they sowed wheat and rye and in the spring hay and oats. At harvest time, a peasant and his entire family, using serrated sickles, would literally have to saw the plants. This meant that one man would cut about two acres a week—not a very efficient technique—and, according to the best estimates of the period, obtain yields of approximately 15 bushels per acre—not a high rate of production.

Besides growing grain for bread and feed, peasants produced fruits, wine, poultry and eggs, and honey. Yet in these endeavors too, work was hard and time-consuming in proportion to yield. This situation prompted the Commerce Department representative in Bordeaux to recommend to his superiors that such agricultural production be encouraged and supported more strongly by the central government.

The peasants, sometimes referred to as "the dregs of society," rarely cultivated any land of their own. Usually, it was the Catholic church, the largest landowner in France, or a rich bourgeois, who held the property. He then would rent it out to a tenant-farmer in payment, in kind or in cash, of a pre-specified rent; the sharecropper, as the name indicates, shared his crop with his landlord, who was also reimbursed for all planting and harvesting expenses. The migrant worker was the most wretched member of the peasant class, since he hired himself out for temporary jobs (mainly at harvest times), was paid by the day, and lived on the road.

Mazarin's predecessor as first minister of France, Armand Jean du Plessis, Cardinal Richelieu (1585–1642). A strong believer in royal absolutism and a bitter opponent of all who sought to challenge the powers of the monarchy, Richelieu once declared: "I have no enemies but those of the State."

Besides being at the mercy of the weather, crop failures, and chaotic prices, the peasant was subjected to a series of taxes and duties. Although they were the ones most able to pay, the clergy, nobility, and bourgeoisie (or middle classes) usually paid no tax. However, peasants were compelled to pay the *taille*, an arbitrary tax on real and personal property, the *gabelle* or salt tax, the *aide* on wine and alcohol, various excise taxes on tobacco and legal documents, road and canal tolls, and the poll tax on every man, woman, and child in the household. The local priest demanded an annual tithe, and to the state and landowner a number of days of free labor (known as *corvée*) was owed, on which peasants might repair roads, bridges, mills, or manor buildings. Furthermore, they were also required to provide room and board to troops, who took full advantage of this "hospitality."

It was no wonder that people with a social conscience, such as the military leader Sébastien de Vauban and the writer Jean de La Bruyère, spoke out against the poverty of so many in the kingdom. "Your people are dying of hunger," Bishop Fénelon would later write to Louis XIV. "All France is nothing more than a poorhouse."

Internal strife gave the Paris Parlement what it saw as an opportunity to increase its power in the kingdom. It wanted to keep laws benefiting the upper classes and the aristocracy, and maintain its own privileges of tax exemption. Members of Parlement, inspired by the recent English revolution, also wanted a constitutional monarchy like Britain's. "It is important to Your Majesty that we become free men, not slaves," one parlementery judge exclaimed. Its other aim was to undermine Mazarin's government, which it felt had become too centralized and powerful. A previous conspiracy against Mazarin in 1643 had ended in failure. Now members of Parlement were further outraged when Mazarin proposed real estate and income taxes, mainly affecting the rich. When the minister wanted to raise revenues for future military campaigns, the Paris Parlement stubbornly refused to approve his budget requests. Their negative vote helped set off a series of civil disturbances and riots, called the *Fronde* (after the stone sling used in street brawls).

During the first rebellion, known as the Parlementary Fronde, several political and financial demands were stated in a July 1648 ultimatum. At first it appeared that Mazarin would yield to the Parlement's demands. But the French military success at Lens came just in time to tilt the situation in Mazarin's favor; he then arrested Pierre Broussel, the outspoken leader of the opposition. Unfortunately for the unpopular Cardinal Mazarin (as a foreigner he was often suspected of treachery by the French), his action only provided the spark for the tinders of revolt. The ensuing uprising forced the government to release Broussel, and in October 1648 it resolved to lower or abolish taxes and to guarantee certain individual freedoms.

But unresolved animosities between Mazarin and the Paris Parlement renewed violence. For their safety, the royal family fled Paris, taking refuge in

A 17th-century engraving showing French peasants treading grapes romanticizes a way of life that was, in reality, both brutal and harsh. In his book *Louis XIV and Twenty Million Frenchmen*, historian Pierre Goubert estimates life expectancy in mid-17th-century France at 21; infant deaths, he writes, were "of less moment than . . . a freak tempest or the death of a horse."

Saint-Germain-en-Laye in early 1649. Only just returned from victories abroad, Louis II de Bourbon, the prince of Condé, and his army were able to smash the parlementary rebels. They signed the Peace of Rueil in March 1649. Mazarin apparently had won out once more.

Drunk with their military triumphs against France's adversaries abroad, and with crushing revolt at home, the prince of Condé and his followers expected political rewards. Mazarin and Queen Anne, fearing the prince's ambitions, decided to stop the war heroes from gaining political advancement. On January 18, 1650, the adventurers were seized: Condé, his brother, Conti, and his brother-in-law, de Longueville, were thrown into prison. This began the second Fronde. Mazarin's plans backfired.

The imprisonment of the Condés helped forge an alliance between many disgruntled nobles and the original *Frondeurs*. A subsequent court intrigue forced Mazarin to release Condé in February 1651,

A 17th-century painting shows a migrant worker cutting hay in a barn. Paid by the day and dependent on seasonal employment, migrant workers constituted the most wretched section of the peasant class in 17th-century France.

and exile himself for his own protection to the German Rhineland. Mazarin did, however, continue to advise the queen and her son in his letters before returning to court in January 1652. He suggested that Anne announce that her son was now old enough to rule. Although Louis assumed the full office of king during the tumult of the Fronde, another 10 years would pass before he would become absolute ruler of France.

On September 7, 1651, the 13-year-old Louis XIV declared his majority, or coming of age, in the chamber of the Parlement of Paris: "Gentlemen, I have come to my Parlement to tell you that in accordance with the law of my state, I am going to take upon myself the management of my government and I hope that the goodness of God will grant that this will be with piety and justice. . . ." Father Paulin, Louis's confessor, described the reaction to Louis's declaration: "How great was the applause of the witnesses, the cries of joy, the striking of drums, and trumpets. . . . Alas, the Prince of Condé did not see the public joy. . . ."

Gaining the support of the elderly, but still dangerous, Gaston of Orléans, Condé led a second rebellion known as the Fronde of Princes. With secret help from Spain they waged an all-out war against the royal arm. As Condé and his allies brought havoc and strife to the countryside the child king lay asleep in the palace while men sometimes stormed into his room at night to be sure he had not been abducted. Again the young king had to flee the capital. Allegiances among the various groups kept changing, however, since none of them had a well-defined program or trusted one another. Because these factions could not band solidly together, Henri Turenne, the commander of the loyalist troops, was soon able to defeat the rebels. With order restored, Louis returned to Paris in the fall of 1652. Less than a year later, the Fronde ended in complete failure with the capitulation of the city of Bordeaux. Mazarin and the king emerged from these disorders all the stronger in their positions, but France had been worn out; the peasants reeled beneath the impact of hunger and unrest.

Born just three years before Louis died, French philosopher Jean-Jacques Rousseau (1712–78) wrote much that would have appalled the Sun King. The ideas of philosophers like Rousseau (who considered the will of the people the only rightful authority) formed the intellectual underpinnings of the republican revolution that was to sweep France at the end of the 18th century.

Riots were common throughout France between 1648, when middle-class opposition to Mazarin and the monarchy erupted into rebellion, and 1652, when the wily cardinal finally regained control of the country following the collapse of the coalition that had been formed between the middle class and the nobility.

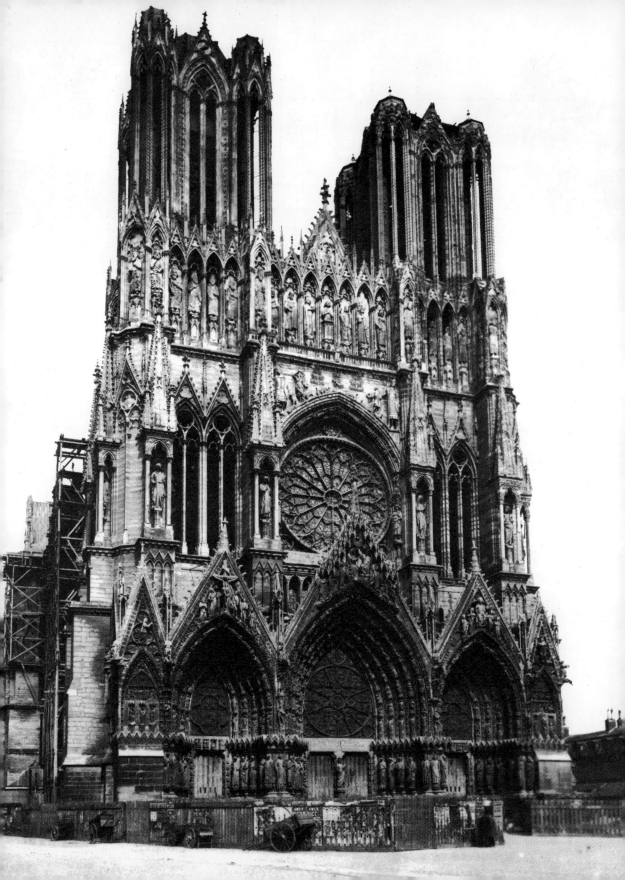

2

The Rising Sun

Louis XIV was rather short by modern standards, 5′5″, but well proportioned, with a graceful and attractive physique. He had a presence that exuded self-assurance and dignity, highlighted by the fact that he was always courteous and polite. The *Gazette de France* stated that even early in his life everyone was impressed by his "perfect beauty," his "maturity," his "confidence beyond his years," and his "dignified carriage." Louis had become everything his mother wished in a son.

Anne had made sure that Louis received a proper education. The boy king had been educated by various private tutors who daily reminded him that "homage is due to kings; they may act as they please." They taught him how to conduct himself as a monarch, and what he should expect from his subjects. When Louis was seven, his first tutor presented him with a book entitled *Catéchisme Royale*, which stated that religion granted the king all his power. He was schooled in little, however, that was useful to a head of state, such as history, finance, or geography. On the other hand, he received an extensive moral education from his mother.

THE BETTMANN ARCHIVE

Oliver Cromwell (1599–1658) was the architect of the parliamentarian victory over King Charles I of England (1600–49) and his royalist supporters in the English Civil War (1642–47). Cromwell approved Charles's execution in 1649 and became his country's Lord Protector in 1653. Four years later he concluded an alliance with Mazarin.

Rheims Cathedral, where Louis was crowned king of France in 1654. Believing that he was directly chosen by God to serve as monarch, Louis felt a personal sense of responsibility for the religious life of all his subjects.

GIRAUDON/ART RESOURCE

She taught by concrete example, and punishment was frequent. For the slightest disobedience Louis was sent to his room. In one instance, he was confined to his room for two days for trying out language that he had heard in the stable. His mother's insistence that he should not take God's name in vain probably formed the basis of Louis's purity of language in later life. Anne's teachings were also apparently responsible for his deep interest in the rituals of the Catholic religion. One clergyman noted: "There is no lamb more sweet, more tractable than our King . . . he had in him the piety which the most Christian Queen has inculcated in him from early childhood."

A king's education would demand more than religious training and a little book learning. From Mazarin, who profoundly understood human nature, he received an excellent training in statecraft. In conversations with foreign ambassadors he could discuss world affairs with surprising competence. According to Mazarin, Louis learned by listening, reading, and doing. From the time Louis was 14,

The coronation of Louis XIV in 1654. Although Louis was not to become absolute ruler of France until March 1661, when he announced his intention to govern without a first minister, his coronation marked the official commencement of his reign.

ALINARI/ART RESOURCE

Mazarin received him each day in his private chambers for a discussion of current problems of state. All this practical instruction helped to shape Louis's attitude toward work and command. It ultimately molded his concept of self, which he would later demonstrate in his style of being, thinking, and ruling. Above all, there was one lesson he learned at an early age: the two revolts, court intrigues, and the humiliation of fleeing the capital, had taught him to trust no one—not even his own family. He built a wall around himself to conceal his real feelings. "Have no attachment to anyone," he once said. Probably more than any other experience, the Frondes convinced Louis that, as king, he must wield absolute power.

Louis's military training was not ignored either. Very early in his life he learned to ride a horse, swing a sword, and fire a musket. Louis had also participated in several battles during the Frondes and studied military strategy and organization in the field under Turenne.

Out of this training came a well-balanced young man, one who was careful and discerning, even slow in his actions. Like his teacher, Cardinal Mazarin, Louis preferred to wait a little longer than to rush into a task. His favorite answer to critics was: "We shall see." Sainte-Beuve, a famous French author of the 19th century, wrote that Louis XIV possessed only common sense, but a lot of it. The king knew how to compensate for his lack of brilliance by hard work, which he performed methodically and with great dedication. His work habits were so consistent it was possible to determine the time of day from his schedule. He also knew how to surround himself with good counselors and ministers, who were chosen mainly from the middle class, and who thought clearly and analytically; he valued the advice of experts and learned from their insight and experience.

Louis enthusiastically supported the arts. A good dancer and actor, he often took part in many of the entertainments staged for his pleasure. During his reign, the playwrights Molière and Racine produced their great works for the stage; artists like Le Brun and Hardouin-Mansart flourished. In Voltaire's

> *God established kings to guarantee the property, the security, and the peace of their subjects, and not to sacrifice any of these for their own individual passions.*
> —JULES MAZARIN
> in a letter urging Louis XIV
> to marry Maria Theresa

words, Louis's era was "the Great Century of a Great Monarch."

Having been treated as a king since his childhood, he came to expect flattery and admiration from all his subjects. He reveled in the magnificent pomp and pageantry used to emphasize his regal grandeur. Court protocol and lavish ceremony reached their pinnacle under Louis. As British historian Alfred Cobban explains, "The object was to provide the necessary setting for a monarch who was to be the centre of the nation with all eyes turned on him. The life of the king passed from birth to death in public." He was, after all, the grandson of Henry IV, the French king who had restored peace after the divisive Wars of Religion; the great-grandson of Philip II, who ruled Spain during her Golden Age; and thus he was also the great-great-grandson of Charles V, emperor of the Holy Roman Empire.

Louis would have considerable time to learn necessary political skills, and observe the state during a deep and prolonged crisis. He was not to become undisputed ruler of France until 1661, when Cardinal Mazarin would be dead and the ill-fated finance minister, Nicolas Fouquet, languishing in prison. In his *Mémoires*, Louis explained the real nature of his majority: "[It is] the age that the laws of France have established to avoid great evils, [but] . . . not that at which private individuals begin to control their own affairs." Mazarin remained in control.

As Mazarin embarked upon rebuilding the country between 1653 and 1661, calm and order replaced unrest and chaos. It was a slow and arduous task, made even more difficult by a series of crop failures, harsh winters, and a depleted treasury. Through his resolve and skill, the cardinal, now frequently sharing the reins of government with the king, managed to restructure the tax-collecting system, to borrow money (at high interest rates), and to alleviate the plight of the poor. Under the able management of the war secretary, Michel Le Tellier, he began reorganizing the army, which would soon be needed against Spain, still belligerent despite its own grave economic problems.

There is in him enough stuff to make four kings and a sensible man.

—JULES MAZARIN
French cardinal and statesman

Maria Theresa of Austria (1638—83), daughter of King
Philip IV of Spain (1605—65), was betrothed to Louis in
1659. Under the terms of their marriage contract, which
was arranged by Mazarin, Maria Theresa agreed to renounce her right of succession to the Spanish throne.

Louis II de Bourbon, prince of Condé (1621–86) bows before Louis XIV. The prince was pardoned by the king for having participated in a rebellion against the monarchy by leading members of the nobility in 1650–52. Condé later led the armies of France to resounding victories over the Spanish and the Dutch.

To achieve his aims, Cardinal Mazarin struck an alliance with Oliver Cromwell in March 1657. England's Lord Protector had good reasons for wanting such an alliance with France: a war would weaken Spain's navy and render her American colonies highly vulnerable to future English invasions. Turenne's French troops, plus 6,000 English soldiers loyal to Cromwell, defeated the Spanish at the Battle of the Dunes on June 14, 1658, and Louis entered Dunkirk in triumph. This victory forced Spain the following year to sign the Treaty of the Pyrenees. France received a sizable portion of Artois in the

In arranging the political marriage, Mazarin anticipated that the Spanish would not be able to afford the huge dowry demanded by France. He reasoned that this could provide Louis with a good excuse for future intimidation of Spain.

north, all of Roussillon (a southern province east of
the Pyrenees), and several fortified towns along the
northeastern frontier. Dunkirk was claimed by England and later sold to France in 1662.

Louis's own marriage was devised to further the
cardinal's extensive plans to increase French political power. In addition to the peace treaty, Mazarin
put together a marriage contract for the French king
and the 22-year-old eldest daughter of the Spanish
king, Philip IV. Maria Theresa was short, plump,
and not particularly pretty but she had a cheerful
disposition. Though he found her boring, Louis al-

This engraving of Louis was commissioned in 1662 to commemorate his assumption of absolute power the previous year. The king's iron determination to tolerate no opposition is well summed up by a statement he made at that time. "For subjects," he declared, "peace lies only in obedience."

ways treated her courteously. For her part, she thought him handsome and charming. An important clause of the agreement stipulated that Maria Theresa would abandon all her claims to the Spanish succession "in consideration" of a dowry of 500,000 gold crowns. Knowing very well that Spain was unable to pay this enormous sum, Mazarin had opened a large loophole that might later be exploited by France in future disputes, and used to gain more territory.

Though Louis had fallen passionately in love with Mazarin's niece, Marie Mancini, and soon made it plain that he wanted to marry her, his mother and the minister proceeded to arrange the more appropriate—and politically advantageous—match with Maria Theresa. In the meantime, a more suitable husband was found for Marie. Recovering from his broken romance, the king then met the lovely and adoring Louise de La Vallière who was overwhelmed by the tender affection he showed her, and she quickly became his mistress. During the next few years she bore him several children (only two survived), but Louis XIV was by then accustomed to the amorous advances of women. When he noticed that Louise had lost much of her beauty, he turned to her friend, the marquise de Montespan. Unable to win her royal lover back, de La Vallière retired in despair to a Carmelite convent.

Still, the wedding between Maria and Louis took place on June 9, 1660, at Fontarabia, a town on the border of France and Spain. The ceremony epitomized royal splendor. Yet it was not to be a happy union for the pair since the king was notoriously disloyal to his wife. The duke of Saint-Simon wrote in his *Mémoires*: "The king was all his life a lover." Indeed, Louis very much enjoyed the company of women, although he did not allow them to interfere in state matters.

Françoise-Athénaïs de Montespan belonged to an old aristocratic family and was often described by her contemporaries as the most beautiful, the most witty and bewitching of all the ladies at court. In contrast to Mademoiselle de La Vallière, Montespan was a statuesque, sensual, and voluptuous woman,

Louis and Maria Theresa's son, Louis le Grand Dauphin (1661–1711), is baptized. Louis, eager to instill in his son the values that he felt befit a king, gave the boy his *Mémoires* (diaries), which stressed "dignity," "glory," "greatness," and "reputation."

Between 1669 and 1679, Françoise d'Aubigné (1635–1719) was governess to the children of Louis's mistress, Françoise-Athénaïs Rochechouart de Mortemart, marquise de Montespan (1641–1707). Madame d'Aubigné eventually replaced Madame de Montespan in Louis's affections and married him in 1684.

who in her relationship with Louis often preferred clever, flippant repartee to a more tactful silence. If at first the king considered her his one true love (he had several illegitimate children by her, whom he recognized and elevated to nobiliary rank, like the duke of Maine), in the end he grew tired of her sharp tongue and shrewd nature.

He soon spent more and more time with their children's governess, Madame Scarron, a minor writer's widow, better known later as Madame "de Maintenon" when Louis gave her the money to purchase a small château in the Eure valley. Realizing how unfeeling and selfish Madame de Montespan truly was, the king declared with a sigh: "Madame de Maintenon knows how to love; there would be great pleasure to be loved by her." Maria Theresa gave birth to only one son who never would reign. Louis called him the Great Dauphin.

While the marriage between Maria and Louis was being arranged, the cardinal was also successfully orchestrating peace settlements between Sweden and Denmark as well as between Sweden, Poland, and Brandenburg, thus preventing Austria's meddling in the Baltic Sea region. (Brandenburg was then a German principality located in what is now central East Germany.) Soon after, on March 9, 1661, Jules Marazin died at 59, a very wealthy man. Thanks to him, Richelieu's goals had been realized: France had become the greatest power in Europe, had been victorious over Spain and the Austrian Empire, and was influential in Germany and northern Europe.

The next day, Louis assembled his cabinet ministers and made his intentions clear: "I have called you together . . . to tell you that up to this moment I have been pleased to entrust the government of my affairs to the late Cardinal. It is now time that I govern them myself. You will assist me with your counsels when I ask for them. . . ."

Louis's courtiers attend a parade at Versailles, the magnificent palace upon which the king ordered work begun in 1661. One of his wife's ladies-in-waiting once described Versailles as the "palace [Louis] designed for his magnificence in order to show by its adornment what a great king can do when he spares nothing to satisfy his wishes."

A 17th-century drawing entitled *Marine and Other Deities Paying Homage to Louis XIV.* Early in his reign, Louis, who believed that his status as king made him God's lieutenant on earth, once declared that he received occasional inspiration "straight from heaven."

3

The Carriage of the Sun

Louis XIV set out to govern a territorially expanded but tattered and war-torn country. He had to reestablish law and order. The king wanted to accomplish this with as little interference from cabinet ministers as possible, and he kept their number to a minimum. Several specialized councils assisted the king in his task. The two most important of these were the Privy Council, the kingdom's highest court, presided over by a chancellor, and the Council of State. The latter was divided into three departments: the Supreme Council, which dealt with major government policy, war, and foreign relations; the Council of Dispatches, which handled internal affairs (including police, public works, and administration); and the Council of Finance, which considered all tax and budget matters.

Many of Louis's ministers had been recommended by Mazarin, particularly Fouquet, Le Tellier, Colbert, and Lionne. Nicolas Fouquet was a very effective, and extremely rich, superintendent-general of finance. It was Fouquet who believed himself the logical choice as the king's next chief adviser, and

THE BETTMANN ARCHIVE

Shortly after assuming absolute power in 1661, Louis expressed his vision of the French monarchy in majestic pronouncements, one of which read: "The kings of France, as hereditary kings . . . may boast that there is without exception in the world today no greater house than theirs, no monarchy as ancient, no greater or more absolute power."

Louis conducts an audience with a representative of Mehmed IV, sultan of the Ottoman Empire (1642–93), in 1669. Louis's vision of himself as a defender of Christendom rarely prevented him from maintaining cordial relations with the Muslim Turks, whose extensive domains he considered an excellent market for French trading interests.

SNARK/ART RESOURCE

it was he who would fall prey to Louis's own jealousy and ambition. Louis did not want to be overshadowed by another first minister; he would rule without one. After Mazarin's death, no longer having a churchman in high office also meant that France would look to the king, not the pope, for leadership. Louis wrote in his *Mémoires* that kings ". . . holding as it were the place of God, we seem to participate in his wisdom as in his authority; for instance, in what concerns discernment of human character, allocation of employments, and distribution of rewards."

> **It is legal because I wish it.**
> —LOUIS XIV

With regard to his counselors, Louis stated: "I wished to divide the execution of my orders among several people, the better to bring them under my authority. It was with this in mind that I chose men of diverse talents and professions, fitting the diversity of the materials that ordinarily fall under the administration of state, and I distributed my time and my confidence according to the understanding that I had of their virtues and the importance of the affairs that I gave over to them."

A song in 1670 described the "carriage of the sun" as being drawn by four horses that "were neither good nor beautiful"—these were Colbert, Le Tellier, Lionne, and Louvois. These men were Louis's personal advisers, and he expected complete secrecy from each of them. In his opinion the king's business was not the business of the rest of the court.

Jean Baptiste Colbert was not only a discreet and fiercely loyal civil servant, but a capable and hardworking minister in whom Louis had complete confidence. In his words he "took no holiday, had no pleasure nor amusement and spent my whole life on the Cardinal's business as what I love is work." He was known for his austere look, and was, in fact, nicknamed the "North" after the cold, sharp wind.

Colbert had been educated as a lawyer and had some experience in banking. He entered the king's service under Mazarin, who, on his deathbed, recommended him to Louis. Shortly after Fouquet's fall, Colbert became the controller-general of finance and in this newly created position was charged with straightening out the chaotic, often unjust, collection of taxes. Under his direction an attempt was made to reform the tax system. Moderately successful in his mission, he was given greater responsibilities and was soon entrusted with the administration of the navy, fine arts, internal affairs, commerce, and industry. In these posts he showed the same breadth of knowledge and judgment as he had in the Finance Department.

An essentially conservative administrator, Colbert built his policies on two assumptions: one was to stop wasteful borrowing (thus lowering the national debt); the other was to encourage commerce and trade as much as possible. He advocated a policy of high tariffs, designed to strengthen production at home and keep foreign, especially Dutch, goods out of France. Colbert believed that a planned economy was vital to accomplishing these ends. But as the government came more and more to direct trade and manufacturing, he found that merchants and colonists who made a profit were not always the result. In addition, his policies depended exclusively upon large monopolies to launch colonies and for-

A 17th-century engraving shows French warships at anchor in the port of Caudebec. The considerable expansion undergone by the French navy and merchant marine during Louis's reign was largely due to the genius of one man—Jean-Baptiste Colbert (1619–83), whom Louis appointed minister of marine in 1669.

eign trade. These oversized companies became increasingly unable to support themselves and collapsed. Colbert's program of strict trade protectionism also helped push France and the Dutch closer to war.

In such a planned economy, workers and farmers had to work harder at producing non-foodstuffs such as hemp, cloth, tobacco, and silk. Craftsmen and engineers were hired from abroad, and newly created industries now competed with foreign concerns in the manufacture of lace, steel, tapestries, mirrors, furniture, cloth, china, and glass. New markets had to be found for French products whether through commercial ties with previously neglected regions of the world (for instance, India and Siam) or through colonization of Africa.

In North America, where Samuel de Champlain had founded the city of Quebec in 1608, the entire province, of the same name, including parts of Maine, was annexed in 1663. Similarly, after Louis

The Wardens of the Amsterdam Drapers Guild, by the great Dutch artist Rembrandt van Rijn (1606–69). Louis's resentment of the Dutch republic's commercial superiority in Europe, combined with his instinctive dislike of its republican form of government, was largely responsible for his decision to go to war with that country in 1672.

Joliet, Jacques Marquette, and René-Robert Cavelier de La Salle discovered and explored the Mississippi region in 1673, the Louisiana Territory (named after Louis XIV) also became French in 1682. Finally, France took Haiti in the West Indies in 1697 and Guiana in South America somewhat earlier.

To aid in this worldwide undertaking and to protect a burgeoning empire, Colbert built a merchant marine and military navy that rivaled those of Britain and Holland. Since he headed the Internal Affairs Department, he improved roads and bridges and had canals dug or widened; he also simplified civil and criminal laws, helped write a code for business, reformed and centralized the police, especially in Paris, and improved the mines and harbors. In addition, he supported the arts and the sciences by creating Academies of Fine Arts, Music, and Science and by setting up the Observatory.

Merchants confer in a northern European port during the 17th century, a period that witnessed ever-increasing competition between the major European trading nations. Under the administration of Colbert, the French merchant marine eventually posed a substantial threat to the commercial supremacy of the Dutch, whom Louis once ridiculed as a nation of "cheese merchants."

With his councillors in attendance, Louis presides at the opening of the Academy of Sciences in 1666. The king's policy of establishing academies financed by royal patronage reflected his determination to ensure that all endeavors in art, literature, and science would glorify his own person.

Michel Le Tellier, Louis's military adviser, had been *procureur du roi* (curator of the king), *maître des requêtes* (master or minister of petitions), and minister of the army under Cardinal Richelieu. Mazarin considered him a trusted adviser and made him secretary of state in charge of military affairs.

Le Tellier was responsible for creating an army that was well trained and efficient. By issuing and enforcing regulations on recruitment, training, discipline, command, supplies, and medical care, he created a formidable military force that answered solely to the crown. One historian said of Le Tellier's reforms: "Between 1655 and 1675 Le Tellier's regulations laid down the basic pattern of the pre-revolutionary Bourbon army; after 1675 new ordinances were never much more than minor revisions of the basic regulations made necessary by the changes in weapons or by abuses in organization. These first decades of Louis XIV's reign set a military pattern both for France and Europe that was to last for generations to come."

Hugues de Lionne, the king's foreign minister, has not been as well remembered as other figures in the 17th century. Although Lionne had helped negotiate both the Treaty of Westphalia and the Peace of the Pyrenees, it appears that he was not a very ambitious man. He seemed content with his unproclaimed title as "expert" on French foreign affairs and wished for nothing more. At 50 years of age, shortly before Mazarin's death, Lionne had become both confidant and adviser to the cardinal. He had a long career as a diplomat and was a subtle and skilled negotiator.

Lionne was also a good judge of character. In August 1661 he made some very acute remarks concerning the intentions of the Sun King: "Those who believe that our master will soon give up the direction of affairs deceive themselves. . . . The more we go along, the more pleasure he [the king] takes in applying himself and giving himself entirely to the affairs of the kingdom." The archives of the Foreign Ministry show that Lionne was indeed a close adviser to the king. When writing the policy of the kingdom, he took carefully into consideration

Louis's personal interests and motives.

The newcomer to the king's council, the son of Le Tellier, and the future minister of war, was François Michel Le Tellier, the marquis de Louvois. Beginning in 1661, he had begun to take over his father's office of secretary of state for war, a position held by the older man since 1643. Like his father, Louvois was a talented government official. In contrast to Le Tellier, however, Louvois was harsh, ruthless, and aggressive. Many historians suggest that his was a sinister influence on Louis.

Louvois completed his father's reorganization of the armed forces by setting up an efficient system to keep frontline troops well supplied with food and ammunition (thus gaining the nickname the "great victualler"). He established cadet and military engineering schools; and introduced the flintlock mus-

Rembrandt's *The Anatomical Lesson of Dr. Tulp* reflects his fascination with the spirit of scientific inquiry, which was a hallmark of the Dutch republic's cultural progress throughout the 17th century. While French scientists were forced to work on Louis's terms, their Dutch counterparts were able to conduct their researches in an atmosphere of relative freedom.

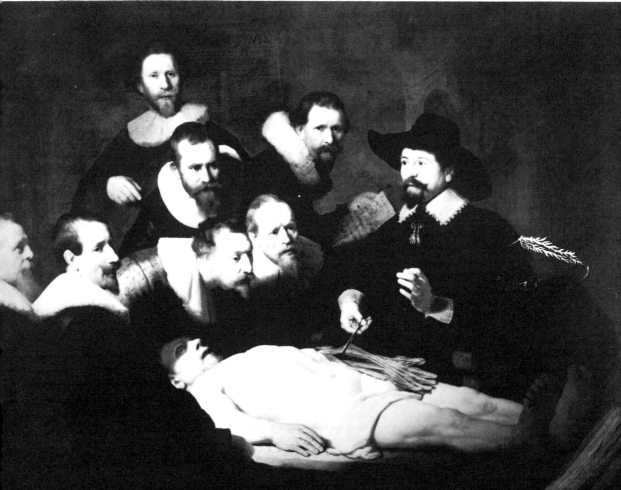

ket. The artillery was upgraded and made an important branch of the service. Finally, to take care of the wounded, he founded a large army hospital in Paris.

In 1672 he unofficially took over the conduct of foreign affairs as well, often counseling an inflexible, even blunt, diplomatic stand that would allow him to use the well-oiled fighting machine he had helped construct and to make himself increasingly indispensable. After the death of Colbert in 1683, Louvois came closer to the role of first minister than any of Louis's advisers.

Louis was often directly involved in military affairs and with the idea that France was embodied in his person, he quickly made it his mission to impose French influence on the continent. This move continued a trend begun when France had dictated the Treaties of Westphalia and the Pyrenees to the warring countries of the Thirty Years' War, thus obtaining many territorial concessions from Austria and Spain. There had also been several battles against the Turks in 1664, won with distinction by the French.

In the 1670s Louis XIV committed his armies to pitched warfare. His militaristic ambition was to be focused on Holland throughout this decade. But the prelude to Louis's furious onslaught against the Dutch was a conflict he had instigated some four years earlier, known as the War of Devolution. This attack on the Spanish Netherlands (modern-day Belgium) was rationalized by Louis through a dispute over his wife's inheritance. Louis's father-in-law, King Philip IV of Spain, died in September 1665; his son by a second marriage was his only heir. The marriage contract between the French king and Maria Theresa had required King Philip IV to pay a dowry to Louis. Philip died without paying it. These marital economics were complicated further by the fact that Maria had renounced all claims to her father's will. Louis was told by his legal advisers that he was still entitled to a dowry totaling 500,000 gold crowns. They also argued that since the dowry was never paid, and because royalty could not legally renounce their inheritance, Louis was

When Louis's armies invaded the Dutch republic in 1672, the outnumbered and under-equipped Dutch compensated for their disadvantage by destroying the dikes, or embankments, that protected their country (much of which lies below sea level) from flooding. Here, Dutch soldiers and civilians work to dismantle a floodgate.

being denied what was rightfully his. In addition, since local inheritance laws gave precedence to children of the first marriage over those of the second, Louis claimed that large areas of Flanders (the contested region of the Spanish Netherlands) must "devolve" to his wife. When Maria Theresa's rather dubious rights were not generally recognized, Louis ordered an expeditionary force totaling 35,000 men into the Low Countries in May 1667; led by Turenne, they took several important northern strongholds while Condé's troops captured Franche-Comté (in east central France) in less than two weeks.

Nevertheless, threatened by the combined forces of England, Holland, and Sweden, known as the Triple Alliance, the king preferred to come to terms and consolidate his gains. He did so on May 2, 1668, by signing the Treaty of Aix-la-Chapelle. Louis neatly settled for acquiring the towns of Charleroi, Douai, and Lille on the Franco-Flemish border. The campaign Louis had waged on Spanish territory had alienated the Dutch. Louis had begun to provide momentum to France's longstanding desire to expand further northward. He was intensely eager to take these possessions out of foreign hands. Giving in to the Triple Alliance would prove to be only a temporary setback for his imperial aims.

Louis had decided to wage war against the Netherlands ever since the Dutch leader Johan de Witt had initiated the Triple Alliance in May 1668. The maritime powers, England and Holland, had dared to join forces against France. Louis viewed the Dutch role in this alliance as meddlesome and insolent. He was outraged that Holland was showing "ingratitude to those who . . . helped to create its republic," and also that it threatened to push France to the earlier boundaries set by the treaties of Westphalia and the Pyrenees. For such a small nation to act as arbiter between five kings was an insult. Louis and his advisers grumbled that a nation run by "cheese merchants" and business interests was not on the same level as one with a monarch who ruled by divine right.

To Louis the Dutch were barely human. Although there were many Protestants in England, King Charles II at least was a Roman Catholic; the Dutch were devoted to Protestantism, and their government was not a monarchy, but a republic. They represented the opposite of everything Louis stood for.

Before launching a full-scale military attack against Holland, diplomatic steps had to be taken against the Triple Alliance. In May 1670 Charles II and Louis negotiated the Treaty of Dover. With this treaty Louis shattered the alliance between England and Holland. Charles II agreed to help the French king in his plan to annihilate the Dutch. In fact, England's fleet would be used to support the French onslaught. In exchange, Charles would receive enough money to help him become less dependent on the English Parliament for his finances. Louis also agreed to give the English the Isle of Walcheren, with its two ports. Sweden's neutrality was bought with new subsidies, and permission was obtained by French armies to cross German territory. Elector Frederick William I of Brandenburg remained a Dutch ally, since he was related to the house of Orange whose Prince William would subsequently drive back the French.

Louis's ministers—Lionne, Colbert, Louvois—were united in the belief that Holland should be punished. They were not merely telling the king what he wanted to hear; each found his own reasons for seeing the value in going to war. Colbert, unlike his militaristic rival Louvois, usually cautioned against armed hostilities because they were expensive gambits. But there were sound economic ends to be served by invading the United Provinces, as the Dutch republic was called. An invasion would logically follow Colbert's anti-Dutch trade policy. The near monopoly Holland held in seagoing transport irritated the finance minister. Only a few years earlier he had asserted, ". . . we must ruin Holland at sea." Louvois claimed that the Spanish Netherlands would never become French until the United Provinces were conquered. Lionne, like the king, believed that the Dutch merchants were "usurpers," who had no right to dictate terms to monarchs.

French merchant ships enter a Mediterranean port during the 17th century. As the French merchant marine expanded throughout the 1670s and 1680s, French trading interests became firmly entrenched in Asia, the Mediterranean, Africa, and the Americas.

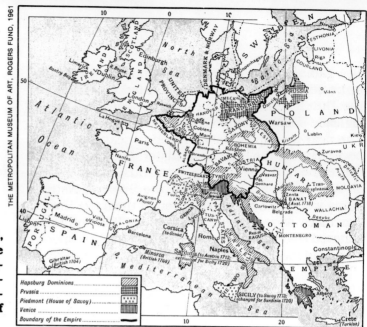

A map of Europe in 1720, with the Holy Roman Empire outlined in bold. The boundaries of France and its neighboring states changed frequently during the wars of Louis XIV's reign.

Lionne died before French armies marched on the little republic.

French troops commanded by Créqui took over Lorraine in August 1670, thus moving into position for the attack on Holland as well as gaining experience in the field. By January 1672 Louvois was made minister of state. Accompanied by his confessor and his historian, who was careful to record events as Louis saw them, the king traveled from Paris to review his vast army.

Louis's desire to conquer—both in love and war—derived from his own insecurity, which was manifest in a deeply rooted need to prove his greatness as a man and a ruler. During the Dutch War, Louis XIV's armies fought not only for political goals, but also to impress the "three queens," as peasants called them: Maria Theresa, Mademoiselle de La Vallière, and the marquise de Montespan. He had insisted on packing all three women into a coach to travel hundreds of miles and watch his war against the Dutch firsthand.

Without a declaration of war, 120,000 soldiers, led by Turenne and Condé, invaded Holland in June 1672; 110,000 of these streamed across the border from nearby Cologne. After meeting at Maastricht, Condé and Turenne set out to cross the Rhine River using specially designed pontoons. The flustered and outmaneuvered Dutch army fell back to defend Amsterdam. Before July the provinces of Overissle and Gelderland were held by the French. Louis soon arrived in Utrecht to reclaim its cathedral for Catholicism.

De Witt, the grand pensionary of Holland, thought defeat inevitable, just as Dutch naval genius de Ruyter was demonstrating that he was more than a match for the English and French fleets at Southwold Bay. As for fighting on land, water would stop Condé and his soldiers from advancing on Amsterdam. To save the capital, the Dutch chose to break the dikes, their ultimate defensive move. As Amsterdam became an island, crops were destroyed and the carcasses of drowned livestock floated in the rising waters. Between the sections of land separating the various canals and rivers, 10,000 Dutch soldiers were at the ready.

Envoys from de Witt were met with peace demands that were exacting to the point of cruelty. Probably influenced by the frequently brutal Louvois, Louis even asked that a Dutch emissary come yearly to his court with a token symbolizing tribute to the monarch's greatness.

As Holland struggled valiantly against the invaders, the Dutch republic was suddenly overthrown in a bloody uprising. On July 8, 1672, the 22-year-old Prince William of Orange, who had been captain-general of the Dutch army since February, was elected *stadholder* (a created office with dictatorial powers). De Witt had had great difficulty unifying his country against France. Several provinces had balked at cooperating with him. Controversy set off by his foreign policy, which had once favored the French, became a serious threat to de Witt; the war he was accused of starting soon finished him. On August 20 he was brutally assassinated.

An implacable enemy of France, William of Orange began at once to unravel Louis's patiently woven alliances, particularly with England. William began to dismantle French diplomacy by inciting the English Parliament against King Charles II. Charles was finally forced to withdraw England from the conflict in 1674. (Three years later William would

The frightful troubles that have desolated Europe for more than twenty years, the blood spilt, the scandals, the ravaged provinces, the cities and towns reduced to ashes, all this [was] caused by that war of 1672. It is the true source of all of France's ills.
—FRANÇOIS FÉNELON
French prelate and writer, on the Dutch War

marry the king's niece, Mary of York.)

Shortly after French forces went in pursuit of the elector of Brandenburg, on the Rhine, William went on the offensive and struck at Charleroi, surprising the French with a bold counterattack. In 1673 the elector of Brandenburg's troops were scattered, finally quitting the fight against the French in June. Condé also defeated William at Seneffe in Flanders in 1674. The elector surrendered, and then later returned to battle only to be beaten once more by Turenne in 1675. In July that same year the siege of Maastricht climaxed in an attempt to capture the town. To the playing of violins, Louis and his courtiers observed the final charge against fortifications.

Suddenly the French war effort suffered a great loss. The brilliant general Turenne was killed at Salzbach on July 27, 1675, during the Alsatian campaign. Condé, whose horse was shot out from under him three times in battle, left his command because of failing health. France continued to score victories, however. On the high seas, Admirals Tourville and Duquesne were able to vanquish the Spanish and Dutch fleets off the coast of Sicily, and easily took Messina. Not even de Ruyter, one of the greatest admirals of the 17th century, could dislodge them; he was wounded in the attempt at Agosta, and died shortly thereafter. On land, numerous fortified towns fell to Louis's forces, and William of Orange, never a very good strategist, was again beaten, this time in 1677, at Cassel by Louis's younger brother.

All belligerents were soon exhausted and interested in peace. Treaty negotiations took place in Nijmegen, Holland, from August 1678 to February 1679. Although she did not receive all the lands she had conquered, France's new territories included Franche-Comté, another section of Flanders, called Hainaut, and the rest of Artois (a sizable portion had come with the Treaty of the Pyrenees), along with the fortress of Freiburg and the duchy of Lorraine.

With the Peace of Nijmegen, Louis's success reached its pinnacle. "I fully rejoice," he wrote in his *Mémoires*, "in my good luck and clever conduct whereby I was able to profit from every opportunity I found to extend the boundaries of my kingdom at the expense of my enemies."

In the summer of 1679, the treaties of Saint-Germain and Fontainebleau were signed to restore to Sweden the lands captured by Holland's hapless allies.

Ironically, the Dutch War might well have ended in a few weeks, but Louvois's ill-conceived ultimatums and uncompromising position toward the de Witt government dragged out the fighting for six years. Yet Louis continued to build upon Cardinal Mazarin's legacy of strong defenses. Moreover, he was able to add the Nijmegen victory to Mazarin's Treaties of Westphalia and the Pyrenees; together, the various annexations ensured greater security along France's border. Louis had proved himself both on the battlefield and at the peace table as the supreme arbiter of Europe. It was no wonder that shortly afterward, in 1680, the city of Paris solemnly conferred the title of "Great" upon Louis XIV.

Louis receives the surrender of the governor of Cambrai on April 21, 1677. Two years after the capture of Cambrai, Louis signed the last of the group of treaties known as the Peace of Nijmegen, whereby France obtained territorial concessions from Spain, the Dutch republic, and the Holy Roman Empire.

Qui pourroit peindre vn Roy si Sage
En vain l'on tire son portrait
Il faloit que Minerue entre prit cet ouurage
Pour le rendre parfait.

4

A Palace for Apollo

Louis always remembered the mobs whose target he had been in his early adolescence. Ever since the Frondes, he regarded Paris as the center of seditious factions and decided early in his reign to move his residence. After moving from the traditional home of the French monarchy, the Louvre palace, on October 7, 1643, the royal family had been living in the Palais Royal, an estate bequeathed to Louis XIII by Cardinal Richelieu. Louis XIV chose to build the palace of Versailles, some 15 miles southwest of Paris. Louis would make Versailles into a place of well-ordered existence and rigid etiquette.

When the anarchy of the Frondes was finally ended, France seemed ready for absolute monarchy. Once beginning his actual reign, Louis would give his nation nothing less. He came to believe that to remain strong and able to maintain order meant the king could brook no compromise, could not share power. Louis realized that many of his subjects had become so rich and influential that they could threaten his rule and, ultimately, the monarchy itself. In order to prevent independent action on their part he molded them into obedient court-

This statuette of a cherub blowing upon a conch shell is one of the many similar pieces that adorn the numerous ornamental groves in the gardens of Versailles, the palace to which Louis relocated his court in 1682.

An angel bears a likeness of Louis, as Minerva (the ancient Roman goddess of wisdom) prepares to paint the king's portrait. The poem inscribed upon the angel's banner translates: "He who would seek to paint a king so wise / Would face an impossible task / Minerva would have to undertake this work / To make it perfect."

THE METROPOLITAN MUSEUM OF ART, GIFT OF THE SENATE HOUSE ASSOCIATION, KINGSTON, NEW YORK, 1952

A detail from a painting of Versailles by American artist John Vanderlyn (1775–1852). The entire work consists of a set of semicircular panels joined together and forming a perfect circle. The painting thus provides a panoramic, 360-degree view of Versailles and the grounds in which it stands.

iers whose livelihoods depended on the king's generosity; whose vanity was reinforced through formal appointments, medals, and titles; and whose very happiness emanated from their being in the royal presence. Versailles, henceforth, would be the ideal setting for this purpose, a permanent monument which by its magnificence would dazzle the entire civilized world.

The small village of Versailles had already been noticed by Louis's father, who built there a small château later incorporated in the grand design. Begun in 1661, construction of the palace of Versailles took more than 50 years, employing at one time 36,000 workers and 6,000 draft horses, and cost a fabulous fortune. The architect Louis Le Vau drew up the general plans for the palace. The architect's work had come to the attention of Louis when the king was a guest of Nicolas Fouquet at the elaborate Vaux-le-Vicomte. Jules Hardouin-Mansart, a brilliant classical architect, developed and modified the original plans to conform to Louis XIV's tastes.

One contemporary explained how the palace was meant to symbolize the Sun King in its every detail: ". . . as the sun is the King's emblem and as the poets confound the sun with Apollo, there is nothing in the superb palace which does not bear relation to that deity. . . ."

With its majestic Garden Front facing the main entrance, flanked on each side by two wing-like extensions, the palace gives the impression of a giant bird about to take flight. Inside the central building, on the second floor, are located the Grand Apartments of the King (a suite of six salons typical of the architecture of the second half of the 17th century), the king's bedroom, and the magnificent Hall of Mirrors. Two hundred and twenty feet long, thirty-two feet wide and forty feet high, the Hall of Mirrors, designed by Mansart, features hundreds of mirrors reflecting both the light shining through the windows and the ceiling decorations, done by Le Brun, relating Louis's glorious history in a series of vividly painted allegories.

Complementing this extraordinary splendor were numerous tapestries, oriental rugs, paintings, marble and bronze vases, armchairs upholstered in red and white silk, crystal chandeliers, and everywhere gold and silver, including an eight-foot-high silver throne in the Apollo room.

Finally, André Le Nôtre's formal gardens, with

Designed by Jules Hardouin-Mansart (1646–1708) (who developed and modified the plans drawn up by Louis Le Vau (1612–70), Louis's first chief architect at Versailles), the chapel at Versailles imitates the chapel built at Aachen (known in French as Aix-la-Chapelle) between 792 and 805 by Charlemagne, king of the Franks (742–814).

This tapestry, entitled *Venus and Adonis*, is one of the
many masterpieces created in the workshops of the Gobelins, the manufacturing concern that Louis commissioned "Royal Makers of Furniture to the Crown".

their flower beds, clipped hedges, statuary (by François Girardon and Antoine Coysevox), terraces, lakes, basins, and waterworks (the Great Basin of Neptune alone has 900 fountains), extend the architectural space as far as the eye can see. The beauty and luxury of the palace of Versailles so entranced all the royalty and dignitaries of Europe that they considered it the eighth wonder of the world, and many wanted to build similar castles—though on a smaller scale.

The inhabitants of Versailles were far removed from the poverty of the French peasants and workers. Louis supported—financially or psychologically—many from the aristocratic class who, by law, were not allowed to work. Although he called the nobility his "right arm" and "the firmest support of the throne," they were in fact without real power, except in the actual conduct of battles. In peacetime,

The gardens at Versailles. Although Louis and his courtiers were generally indifferent toward the sufferings of the workmen involved in the construction of Versailles, some of the king's intimates had occasional fits of conscience: one of Louis's mistresses once called Versailles "a favorite without merit."

to keep all these idle people busy and amused at all times, many ceremonial activities that flattered the vain courtiers—as well as the king—were introduced. And, of course, gambling, balls, hunts, feasts, concerts, operas, and theater helped to fill the monotonous days. Thus musicians, writers, actors, and singers took up permanent residence in Versailles, specifically to entertain the king and his

Louis and his courtiers attend a ball at Versailles, where Louis decided to seclude himself in 1682. Some historians have attributed his isolation there as a major reason for the lack of realism that came to characterize his policies.

THE BETTMANN ARCHIVE

François Couperin (1668–1733), the eminent French composer whom Louis appointed director of court music in 1701, was one of the many outstanding musicians who entertained the king and his entourage at Versailles.

court. Chief among these artists were Couperin, Lully, Molière, La Fontaine, and Racine.

While François Couperin was the leading French composer for orchestra and harpsichord, Jean-Baptiste Lully was the master of French opera. Unlike Italian operatic style, French composers stressed the chorus over the more emotional form, the aria. Having become a composer and conductor in Louis's court in 1652, Lully felt that musical events should be enchanting spectacles. He is credited with inventing the operatic introduction called the overture, a form later adopted by composers such as Mozart and Rossini. Lully also composed a dozen operas and incidental music for the plays of Molière, who, due to his energy and many talents (he wrote,

When the great comic actor and playwright Jean-Baptiste Poquelin (1622–73)—who is known to history as Molière—gained Louis's patronage in 1665, he and the troupe of actors that he had led became known as the King's Comedians. Louis thought so highly of Molière that he chose him to be godfather to his first child.

acted, directed, and produced), was the most celebrated artist to enjoy Louis XIV's patronage.

After spending almost 15 years on the road, Molière and his company were noticed by the court when the company performed several hilarious farces. Under the king's patronage, Molière wrote some 30 comedies that satirized—often sharply—social foibles and human shortcomings. For instance, he dealt with hypocrisy in *Tartuffe*, frankness and insincerity in *The Misanthrope*, greed in *The Miser*, and snobbish vanity in *The Would-be Gentleman*. He died, age 51, on stage during the fourth performance of his *The Imaginary Invalid* in 1673. The characters he presented are both individual and universal: they make us laugh at their ridiculous behavior but they also force us to think

An illustration from an 18th-century edition of Molière's 1670 drama *Le Bourgeois Gentilhomme* (*The Would-be Gentleman*). The play satirized the fact that many members of the French *bourgeoisie* (middle-class merchants and manufacturers) were then attempting to buy their way into the aristocracy.

about our own. Like Molière, Jean de La Fontaine concentrated on human emotion and character in his well-known fables. In these satirical tales of animals in human situations he offered practical lessons in allegorical form.

Louis and his courtiers attend a dramatic performance in a courtyard at Versailles.

In the tragic genre, Jean Racine was the uncontested genius. From his first success (*Andromache*, 1667) to his greatest masterpiece (*Phèdre*, 1677) to his last tragedies (*Esther*, 1689, and *Athalia*, 1691) he portrayed heroines, abandoned by God or the

A bust of Louis XIV by Coysevox, who achieved fame not only for his renderings of his royal patron but also for outstanding busts of Richelieu, Mazarin, and the prince of Condé.

gods, driven by a fatal passion that destroys the men they love and, ultimately, themselves. These works exemplify the French classical theater.

Painters and sculptors also added their art to life at Versailles. Among them were Charles Le Brun, Philippe de Champaigne, and Hyacinthe Rigaud. Le Brun, first painter of the king and director of the Royal Academy of Painting and Sculpture, decorated the palace's ceilings. Influenced by the Dutch painters Van Dyck and Rubens, Champaigne is mainly known for his realistic portraits of Richelieu and Colbert. Rigaud's painting of Louis XIV, probably the best representation of the king in all his grandeur, distinguishes his artistic efforts.

Some of the sculptors were Pierre Puget, François Girardon, and Antoine Coysevox. The king had Puget's violent *Milo of Crotona* placed in his garden and later set across from it another sculpture by Puget, titled *Perseus Delivering Andromeda*. Girardon created several groups of statues (*Apollo Attended by the Nymphs*, *Nymphs at their Bath*, *The Abduction of Proserpine*). More than half of the decorative sculptures inside the palace and many busts of bronze and marble, such as those of Condé and the king as a Roman emperor, were the work of Coysevox.

In this huge army of artists should be included all the gardeners who took care of acres of lawns and thousands of flowers, the designer who created the outfits worn at costume balls and other gala events, such as "The Pleasures of the Enchanted Isle" which lasted seven days, and the pyrotechnicians who put on magnificent fireworks displays.

In addition to all the work taking place at Versailles, vast urban projects were undertaken in the provinces, and especially in Paris. These included the Grand Boulevards, adorned by two arches of triumph celebrating French victories in the Rhine valley at Saint-Denis in 1672 and Saint-Martin in 1674, the Royal Bridge designed by Jacques Gabriel in 1685, the Louis-le-Grand Square or the Place Vendôme, today, and Victory Square. The Tuileries Gardens, landscaped by Le Nôtre, were planted, and the Louvre acquired a monumental colonnade.

New churches were built, along with hospitals and colleges.

Obviously, many of those who collaborated on Versailles were also active in Paris: Girardon contributed statues for Cardinal Richelieu's tomb (Church of the Sorbonne), while a number of private mansions were designed by Le Vau and Hardouin-Mansart. Thus did Louis XIV, constantly compared to Apollo, the sun god, know Versailles and Paris to be worthy of his eminence and his glory.

Louis attends the unveiling of a statue in the grounds of Versailles. Among the many great sculptors who worked for Louis at Versailles were Pierre Puget (1620–94), Antoine Coysevox (1640–1720), and François Girardon (1628–1715).

5

Scorched Earth

*There is no doubt that it is
the intention of the king of
France to make himself
master of Europe.*
—PRINCE WILLIAM OF ORANGE
later England's King William III

Just as the phrase "in consideration of a dowry" in his marriage contract had given Louis XIV justification for seizing land in the War of Devolution, the Treaties of Westphalia and Nijmegen had awarded France several territories "with their dependencies," a clause that needed judicial clarification. For the purpose of investigating these legal and historical claims the king decided to convene courts, called Chambers of Reunion, in Lorraine, Metz, Franche-Comté, Flanders, and Alsace. Not surprisingly, the French magistrates decided in France's favor.

During the *Reunion*, spanning the period from 1679 to 1684, Louis was able to collect further possessions for his European empire without much bloodshed. At probably no other time in his reign did Louis enjoy such freedom from interference. Charles II had been paid to remain neutral; William III, the prince of Orange, was at odds with his own government in the United Provinces; and Emperor Leopold of Austria was menaced by the Turks. To make certain that the Austrian emperor, who was principally involved, accepted their verdict, Louis's armies captured Strasbourg in a few days, forcing

THE BETTMANN ARCHIVE

Ottoman Turkish Grand Vizier Kara Mustafa (1634–83) was executed on the orders of Sultan Mehmed IV for having failed to capture Vienna, Austria, despite having forces that greatly outnumbered those of the Catholic kings and princes opposing him. Louis's failure to send French troops to help defend Vienna earned him the hatred of millions of European Catholics.

Louis at prayer. From 1680 onward Louis became increasingly determined to make Catholicism his country's state religion. In 1685 he revoked the Edict of Nantes, which had given France's Huguenot (Protestant) community a number of civil and religious liberties. As a result of the religious persecution that followed, thousands of Huguenots fled the country, some venturing as far as North America.

GIRAUDON/ART RESOURCE

77

its capitulation on September 30, 1681. Thus began another campaign on behalf of Louis's growing empire. Casale, in the Italian Piedmont, was also occupied the same day. Strasbourg, on the Rhine River between Paris and Vienna, and Casale, on the Po River between Turin and Milan would be important strategic cities in any future war plans.

These lightning conquests caused alarm in the other European countries, who were either unwilling or unable to retaliate in order to restrain Louis. This was especially true of Emperor Leopold I, leader of the Austrian monarchy. These quick takeovers probably could not have been better timed. Leopold was then facing both rebellion against Austrian rule in neighboring Hungary and an invasion by Muslim armies. Austria was a Catholic nation, and the Hungarians, many of whom were Protestants, wanted religious and political freedom. The Hungarian revolt encouraged the Turkish invaders, while the rebels in turn were reluctant to interfere with the Turks. Seeing an opportunity to damage the Austrian empire, Louis gave money to the Hungarian nationalists, asking them to join an alliance with France.

The Turkish grand vizier, Kara Mustafa, laid siege to Vienna in July 1683. Without armed Polish intervention on September 12, the Austrian capital would certainly have fallen to the Turks. Louis used this diversion to seize Spanish Luxembourg in June 1684. Early in 1684, French guns pounded the Republic of Genoa for six days, leveling half the city, as punishment for supposedly helping the Spanish, and when longtime ally the elector of Brandenburg showed impatience with the French, Louis applied diplomatic pressure to bring him into line.

On August 15, 1684, after brief negotiations, Austria and Spain signed a truce with France at Ratisbon, Bavaria, agreeing to recognize for 20 years France's new annexations. Armed force combined with clever diplomacy had worked again to increase the territorial holdings of Louis XIV. He was at the height of his power.

A bishop and religious thinker named Jacques-Bénigne Bossuet helped contribute to the theory

Poor woman, it's the only time she has ever given me any trouble.

—LOUIS XIV
on the death of his wife,
Queen Maria Theresa

behind Louis XIV's absolute monarchy. Gallicanism had been a 16th-century French doctrine which held that church and king were separate and independent. Most French bishops felt that their loyalty was divided between the pope in Rome and the king. Members of the Parlement wanted total independence from the papacy. When Louis became king, many in France thought that the king, rather than the pope, should lead the church. Louis tried using a royal power, granted under certain conditions in the past, to appoint bishops and other church officials. To settle the ensuing dispute, an assembly of French clergymen met in 1682. This assembly adopted principles that reflected the ideas of Bossuet, who did much to advocate Louis's absolutist rule. The Gallican Articles (named after the Gallican church) said that kings did not answer to

Louis was not the first French leader to persecute the Huguenots. In 1572 thousands of Huguenots were slaughtered in Paris, probably on the orders of Catherine de Médicis, the queen mother (1519–89). The event—a scene from which is portrayed here— is known to history as the St. Bartholomew's Day Massacre.

the church on nonspiritual matters. While the pope refused to accept these articles, Louis was not forced to nullify them, and he was able to keep his right to appoint vicars.

At about the same time, a dispute arose between Pope Innocent XI and Louis XIV over the election of the archbishop of Cologne. In exchange for renouncing his sister-in-law's claims to the German state on the Rhine, the Palatinate (she was a Palatinate princess by birth), the king demanded that Cardinal von Fürstenberg be endorsed for the Cologne post. When Innocent XI confirmed the prince of Bavaria instead, Louis advised sending troops to seize the pontifical city of Avignon in southern France as well as invading Germany. There, the French troops conquered most of the Palatinate, burned the crops, and sacked Speier, Heidelberg, Worms, and Mannheim in 1689. A bitter outcry went up in Germany against these scorched earth tactics. Pamphlets publicized the savage deeds of French troops and Louis was denounced as a barbarian.

Such acts of devastation, in addition to stories of atrocities told by French Protestant refugees, meant that the absolutist king ruling from his fabulous palace of Versailles had to be stopped. What had started for Louis as the legitimate desire for secure borders had become an inalienable right of conquest, and would now lead to yet another war. This war would last nine long years, leaving most of the participants impoverished.

At this time, the *Grand Monarque*'s royal government began once more to change. After more than 20 years of faithful and outstanding service to the king, during which tax collection had improved and public revenues tripled (though still insufficient to cover the enormous war expenditures and ever-growing budget deficits), Colbert died exhausted at age 64 in 1683. This left Louvois supreme minister, with disastrous results. Queen Maria Theresa's death that same year precipitated even greater change.

Now a widower, but still vigorous, Louis could marry—albeit secretly—his longtime mistress, Madame de Maintenon. Thereafter, there were no more adulterous liaisons with official mistresses, peasant girls, actresses, noble ladies, or chambermaids. The king, now 45, had reformed. Under the stern influence of his new wife and influential members of the clergy, he had begun to worry about his soul.

The atmosphere of the court reflected Louis's change in attitude. The wild festiveness of early Versailles gave way to a perfect model of domesticity. Louis was now a paragon of religious virtue. Madame de Maintenon wrote in 1681: "The King is beginning to think seriously of his salvation, if God preserves his life, there will soon be only one religion in his kingdom."

Born into a Protestant family and converted at age 15 to Catholicism, Madame de Maintenon was very interested in governmental and educational affairs, and also was one of the most cultivated women in the realm. Although she probably never actually pushed her husband to move against the Huguenots (or French Protestants), both her animosity toward them and her strict moral attitude were deeply felt. These feelings doubtless influenced the king's repressive policies and his decision to establish Catholicism as the only state religion. Louis believed in the axiom established under Louis XII, "one faith, one law, one king." Louis refused to tolerate what he came to think had become a "State within a State."

During Louis's reign, acts of persecution against the heretics or followers of the so-called "Reformed Religion" had occurred well before they were officially sanctioned. Schools were shut down, mixed marriages forbidden, and certain trades and professions were closed to Protestants. Starting in 1680, Louvois's dragoons (mounted musketeers) began to terrorize and torture with impunity those who refused to convert. The king would not heed military adviser Vauban's sensible suggestion that "force will never make a true Catholic." These soldiers were so effective that in six weeks during the autumn of 1685 entire Protestant regions seemed to go over to Catholicism.

In 1598 one of Louis's royal forefathers, Henry IV,

In France, the nation does not form an entity: it resides entirely in the person of the king.
—LOUIS XIV

Louis turns to Madame de Maintenon for advice while conferring with his ministers. The extent to which de Maintenon influenced Louis has been the subject of much debate among historians, some of whom believe that her fanatical hatred of Protestants may have accounted for the extreme severity of the king's persecution of the Huguenots.

had granted the Protestants a number of civil and religious liberties under the Edict of Nantes. But now after so many "spontaneous" conversions, Louis saw fit to scrap the old decree and abolish what rights the Protestants possessed. Louis signed the revocation of the Edict of Nantes, which became effective on October 22, 1685.

Under the revocation, all Protestant meeting places were to be destroyed, all Protestant services terminated, Protestant schools closed, and those born into the forbidden faith forced to submit to Catholic baptism. The order was carried out with terrible force. Men were tortured, women flogged, and Protestant ministers caught trying to hold religious services were executed. Thus, with one stroke of the pen, Henry's grandson had abrogated the human rights of a sizable minority, as much, he felt, for the glory of God as for his own. Over time, this arrogant disregard for personal values would prove a bad political blunder, with serious repercussions for France.

During the next 30 years, between 200,000 and 400,000 Huguenots left France, illegally and at great risk to their families and themselves, taking with them their learning, experience, capital, and energy. They emigrated to Holland, Prussia, England, and America. In America they settled in the Carolinas, in Virginia, in New England, and in the New York area. (Not until 1801, under Consul Napoleon Bonaparte, did the Protestants regain their legal status in France.) Moreover, their mistreatment aroused the anger of their co-religionists in Europe, who were shocked by the king's merciless intolerance. Indeed, the Huguenots who fled their fatherland even went so far as to propose a holy crusade against the monarchy.

As for those who remained in France, they waged a series of armed insurrections against the king. Louis therefore was often required to transfer troops from the front to the southern region of the Cévennes Mountains, where they encountered fierce resistance from the rebels (called "Camisards" for their white shirts) led by a 20-year-old Huguenot named Jean Cavalier. Years of guerrilla fighting did

He had a ruthless side to his nature, especially when he was young. This came partly from lack of imagination and partly because he thought it was his duty to uphold the dignity of God's representative on earth.
—NANCY MITFORD
British historian

not dampen Protestant fervor. On August 21, 1715, a provincial synod met in a quarry to reorganize churches for the Camisards and to name new pastors for the faithful.

In response to this repression—partly out of fear and partly out of insecurity—Protestant and Catholic countries alike formed a defensive coalition in 1681, whose only goal was to enforce the accords of Nijmegen and Ratisbon upon an increasingly unyielding Louis.

Now that the Edict of Nantes was no more, and the persecution of the Protestants was in full swing within France, neighboring Protestant states feared

Louis meets with his councillors. Defending his policy of appointing noblemen to his high council Louis once wrote: "It was not in my interest to take subjects of a higher degree. . . . It was necessary that they should entertain no higher hopes for themselves than I might be pleased to gratify."

A portrait depicts Louis's strength of character, which was more than matched by his physical strength. Louis, who has been described by historian Pierre Goubert as a "tireless huntsman, warrior, dancer, gormandizer and lover," often worked for as long as 16 hours a day.

another war was coming. They understood that Louis was not about to limit military activity to his own borders. He soon forced the duke of Savoy (in southeastern France) to take action against the Protestants in the region under his jurisdiction.

Meanwhile, in England, James II had succeeded his brother on the throne and was confident of continued French support in his attempt to restore Catholicism in his kingdom. This might well have been accomplished had it not been for the relentless Prince William of Orange. In November 1688, following a bloodless revolution, William landed in

Devonshire, England, to be crowned King William III, and James was forced to escape to France. Now governed by France's archenemy, England too would join with Austria, Spain, Sweden, Holland, and Bavaria in the League of Augsburg.

Established in the summer of 1686, the League of Augsburg was ostensibly intended to preserve the Peace of Westphalia. However, the alliance was actually devised to oppose Louis XIV, and this pact would form the origins of the later Grand Alliance against him. Louis's aggressive foreign policy was leading to his eventual downfall. As determined as he had always been to make France supreme in Europe, neighboring states became equally determined to topple him.

England's King William III (1650–1702) and Queen Mary II (1662–94) gained their thrones because Mary's father, James II (1633–1701), had attempted, with much encouragement from Louis, to restore Catholicism to England. James was deposed in 1688.

6

The Grand Alliance

Ultima ratio regum.
(The final argument of kings.)
—motto engraved on
Louis XIV's cannons

In reaction to Louis XIV's schemes in western Germany, the two most influential members of the League of Augsburg, the Austrian empire and Holland, signed in May 1689 a defensive and offensive treaty against France to force her to return to the frontier lines drawn by the Treaties of Westphalia and of the Pyrenees 30 and 40 years before. As soon as practical, William of Orange's government joined the alliance in December of 1689, along with Spain, Savoy, and Saxony. Therefore, it became imperative for France that James II, deposed king of England, be restored to the throne so as to disrupt the Grand Alliance's plans. This Louis tried to accomplish, first by supporting James with men and materials in Ireland where the latter had been acclaimed as liberator. Soon thereafter, Admiral de Tourville defeated the English and Dutch navies off Beachy Head in July 1690, but James was beaten at the Boyne River and forced to flee once more to France. In July 1691 Louvois died, and Louis decided to take command of the military. A year later, in a failed attempt to invade England, the French fleet inflicted heavy losses on Admiral Russell, but was itself nearly destroyed at La Hogue. Even so, it was able to make a comeback and sink 90 ships, including

THE BETTMANN ARCHIVE

In 1707 Vauban, Louis's best military engineer, angered his king when he wrote a treatise entitled *Plan for a Royal Tithe*. Vauban's plan called for a single tax that would apply to all social classes and place more of the tax burden on the shoulders of the nobility. Despite years of loyal service to Louis, Vauban was dismissed for his reformist ideas.

A 17th-century engraving shows Louis and his military engineers dressed as ancient Roman soldiers and studying architectural plans for fortifications. Passionately interested in military affairs throughout his life, Louis greatly enjoyed attending maneuvers, participating in parades, and supervising sieges in person.

SNARK/ART RESOURCE

On May 22, 1692, at the Battle of La Hogue, a combined Anglo-Dutch fleet commanded by Admiral Edward Russell (1653–1727) gained a resounding victory over the French navy. The French defeat was largely of Louis's making; he had ordered his fleet into action against a force more than twice the size of his own.

eight war vessels, at the battle off Lagos, in Portugal, on June 28, 1693.

On land, Louis took Mons, a fortress in the Spanish Netherlands, in 1691, and Vauban took Namur in Flanders the next year. By winning a series of battles against the allies, the marshal de Luxembourg proved himself a worthy successor to the famed prince of Condé. He crushed the prince of Waldeck in 1690 at Fleurus. In 1693 he defeated William at Steenkirk and at Neerwinden, where he captured 15,000 prisoners and numerous cannons, and sent them to Paris Cathedral along with so many enemy flags that he was nicknamed "the decorator of Nôtre Dame." In Italy, Nicolas Catinat's troops defeated the duke of Savoy in 1693. In Spain the duke of Vendôme captured Barcelona. Even with all these victories, Louis could not break the military deadlock.

At home, meanwhile, food shortages were commonplace, and years of war had drained the French treasury. Many angry Protestants who had remained on French soil incited riots and agitated in support of Holland and England. The allies were also exhausted, lacking both the finances and the will necessary to fight another long war. Thus in 1696, when Louis offered peace to Savoy, Duke Victor Amadeus readily agreed. The duke was all the more willing to accept a truce since, in exchange for his neutrality, the city of Nice and a portion of Piedmont were to be returned, including Casale and the Pignerol Fortress (where Fouquet had died a prisoner). Within a year, France proposed a general working paper to the other combatants. The French stated that the Treaty of Nijmegen should provide the basis for negotiations instead of the earlier Treaties of Westphalia and the Pyrenees of 1648 and 1659. As a result, France returned all the lands conquered or annexed since 1679, except Strasbourg, and also accepted the principle of a "barrier" of strongholds to defend the Dutch frontier. Finally—and just as important—Louis abandoned James and recognized William as the legitimate king of England. On this understanding, the Peace of Ryswick was signed by all the powers in the fall of 1697.

> *In every treaty, insert a clause which can easily be violated, so that the entire agreement can be broken in the case the interests of the state make it expedient to do so.*
>
> —LOUIS XIV
> from his instructions to a
> French diplomat

No sooner had the ink dried on those documents than the next conflict emerged—the War of the Spanish Succession. This conflict came about because Charles II, the king of Spain, was very ill and close to death. Among the heirs who had the best claims to the Spanish throne were Louis and Maria Theresa's grandson, Philip of Anjou. The other was Archduke Charles, son of Emperor Leopold of Austria.

Charles II's impending death made England, the German states, and the United Provinces tremble. Whether Spain fell to either the Bourbon dynasty of France or the Hapsburg dynasty of Austria, all Europe would be seriously destabilized. Holland and the German states worried about Protestantism's fate if Louis were to command the Spanish crown. England and the United Provinces feared that their

French Lieutenant General Nicolas Catinat (fifth from left; 1637–1712) supervises the bombardment of Montmélian, a city in Savoy, in 1691. A year earlier Savoy's ruler, Duke Victor Amadeus II (1666–1732), had infuriated France by joining the League of Augsburg, an anti-French alliance established in 1686 by Sweden, the Holy Roman Empire, and several German principalities.

Plus on a de moyens, plus on en veut auoi
Ce pauure apporte tout, bled, fruit, argent, sala.
Ce gros Milord assis, prest a tout receuoi
Ne luy veut pas donner la douceur dune euill.

a la mouch
qui volle
il ne faut
point dais

Il faut
paier ou
agreer.

A tous
Seigneurs
tous
honneurs.

Maigre
comme vn
leurier
datache

Le Noble — est l'airaignée et
45 le Paisan la mouche.

Plus a le Diable,
plus il en veut auoir.
I. laguiet ex.

A 17th-century French cartoon compares the relationship between the nobleman and the peasant to that which
exists between a predator—symbolized here by a spider—
and its prey—symbolized by a fly.

commercial ties with Spain would be taken over by France. Dutch security would be no better off with the Spanish Netherlands in Austrian hands and the Emperor Leopold at their border.

William III, English king and former *stadholder* during the Dutch War, urged compromise—although he knew war was inevitable. He counseled Louis that Spain be split three ways among Archduke Charles, Emperor Leopold's son; Joseph Ferdinand, electoral prince of Bavaria; and Philip, Louis's grandson. Leopold was prepared to go to war over the succession. Louis, hoping for a peaceful solution to the crisis, signed the first treaty of Spanish partition in October 1698. The dying Charles made his will, naming Joseph Ferdinand sole heir. But the prince of Bavaria died shortly thereafter. Until his death Charles resisted all suggestions to break up Spain's empire. A second treaty of partition was signed in June 1699 by Louis and William. Just as with the first treaty, Emperor Leopold refused to endorse this new agreement to partition Spain.

Spain possessed territories in Flanders and in Italy, most of South America, as well as Florida, many of the Caribbean islands, and the Philippines in the Pacific. In September 1700 Charles at last made a will leaving everything to Philip, the duke of Anjou, Louis's grandson, with the express requirement that he could never be king of Spain and king of France at the same time. Charles died on November 1, 1700. Later in November, Louis XIV brought the 17-year-old duke before the assembled courtiers and diplomats at Versailles, and proclaimed: "Gentlemen, here is the king of Spain."

This seemingly fortunate turn of events so intoxicated Louis that he unwisely declared to the Parlement of Paris that the duke of Anjou, to be known as King Philip V of Spain, retained his rights to the French throne. Having already violated Charles's will, Louis decided to govern the Spanish colonies for the benefit of French commercial interests and to invade the "barrier" towns defending the Dutch frontier. French troops entered Flanders, taking Antwerp on their way toward Holland. As if these

> *Louis XIV did more good for his country than twenty of his predecessors together.*
> —VOLTAIRE
> French philosopher

acts were not galling enough, he further provoked the English by recognizing James III as king of England on the death of the exiled James II in September 1701. At the insistent urging of King William, Austria and Holland joined the Grand Alliance of 1701 and thus united with him against France. William died on March 19, 1702, before hostilities began. He had nevertheless created a formidable coalition that would ultimately restrict France's power for a century.

France's allies at this stage were few and would become fewer: while Bavaria remained loyal despite disagreements with Versailles, Portugal and Savoy quickly switched sides and joined the Grand Alliance; Brandenburg was already supporting the alliance against France; Spain was bankrupt.

At first the French forces, led by the daring officer Villars, were victorious at Friedlingen in 1702 and Höchstädt in 1703. Reverses soon followed, however, caused as much by the incompetence of French generals as by the brilliance of their adversaries. Unlike previous conflicts, this time England and Austria had in John Churchill, duke of Marlborough, and in Prince Eugene of Savoy two great field commanders, backed by the skilled English navy. The port of Gibraltar surrendered to the English fleet in three days on August 1704, and Barcelona capitulated to Archduke Charles, who also conquered Valencia and Murcia.

In Germany, Marlborough crushed the Franco-Bavarian army at the Battle of Blenheim in Bavaria during the summer of 1704. Two years later, the struggle stretched from Germany and Flanders to Spain and Italy. French troops were routed at Ramillies in Belgium and outside Turin, Italy, followed by panicky retreats. France suffered two major defeats at Oudenarde and Lille in the late summer and fall of 1708, again against the duke of Marlborough. By 1709, a terrible year for France with subfreezing cold temperatures and widespread famine, Louis XIV, influenced by the defeatist party led by Madame de Maintenon, was ready to discuss peace.

He agreed in principle to remove the young King Philip from the Spanish throne, return Alsace and

The present war is a struggle for the commerce of the Spanish Indies and the riches which they produce.
—LOUIS XIV
on the
War of the Spanish Succession

Strasbourg to the emperor, and take down fortifications in Dunkirk. But when the allies demanded he use the military to expel his grandson, he replied: "I would rather make war on my enemies than on my children."

As a consequence, French resolve stiffened and fighting continued that summer, ending in the Battle of Malplaquet, September 11, 1709, where Villars's army resisted gallantly and fiercely against Marlborough and Eugene. In spite of the allies' victory, it had been hard won (they lost 23,000 men). Thus, their planned invasion of France was thwarted. In Spain, with fresh reinforcements, the duke of Vendôme succeeded in defeating the British and Austrians at Brihuega and at Villaviciosa in December 1710.

At about the same time, a new government came to power in London and sued for peace—all the more vigorously since the sudden death of Holy Roman Emperor Joseph I in April 1711 made the Archduke Charles his successor. Both the Austrian and Spanish crowns would be his if victory went to the allies. In England, Queen Anne's ministers, having no desire to create another Holy Roman Empire, promptly signed the first draft of a peace accord, known as the Preliminaries of London. Such a treaty was being discussed in Utrecht and was finally signed

English marine artillery in action during the opening stages of the War of the Spanish Succession (1701–14). The conflict resulted when Louis approved the declaration made by King Charles II of Spain (1661–1700) that Louis's grandson Philip, duke of Anjou (1683–1746), should succeed him on the Spanish throne.

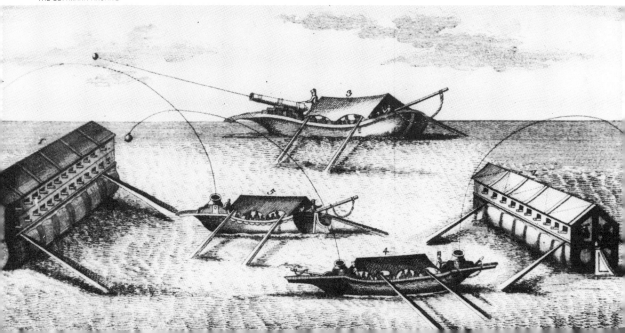

An early 18th-century drawing glorifies Louis's reputation as a military genius. This reputation—along with his army's reputation for virtual invincibility—suffered a terrible blow in 1704, when a combined English, German, and Savoyard army inflicted 20,000 casualties upon a 56,000-strong French force at Blenheim.

in 1713 by all parties except the inflexible archduke, now Emperor Charles VI, who hoped by one decisive blow to extract greater concessions from Louis XIV.

After Prince Eugene had besieged the town of Landrecies in trying to invade France proper, Villars was dispatched to stop him. Tricking the Austrians into thinking that he would attack there, he met them instead 20 miles to the east at Denain, on the Scheldt River, and defeated them soundly on July 24, 1712. Napoleon would later remark that the battle "saved France." This morale-boosting French victory, plus several more the following year on the left bank of the Rhine, convinced the new Austrian emperor also to negotiate an honorable settlement in Rastadt, on March 6, 1714.

This time the terms of the treaties were acceptable to Louis and his allies. King Philip V of Spain and his descendants renounced the French crown, and the French royal princes renounced "eternally and forever" their Spanish claim. In addition, Philip was required to surrender Gibraltar to the British, along with substantial trading privileges in South America. He also gave up Sicily to Duke Victor Amadeus and Milan, Naples, and Belgium to Austria (these heavily mortgaged), but he was confirmed on his throne. Lost lands were restored to Bavaria.

France received Lille, Strasbourg and Alsace back, but had to return Nice, Savoy, parts of Belgium, and

A French merchant fleet arrives at the Caribbean island of Martinique during the late 17th century. By 1500 France's merchant marine was conducting operations as far afield as South America, India, and China.

the southern Rhineland, conquered during the long campaign. The far-flung possessions in North America, Newfoundland, Acadia (Nova Scotia), and Hudson Bay Territory in Canada were also ceded to Great Britain. Important, too, for future political and military developments were European confirmation of the elector of Brandenburg as king of Prussia, and Louis's recognition of the Protestant House of Hanover in London at the expense of the Catholic Stuarts. Thus the 11-year War of the Span-

Louis's courtiers attend a pageant at Versailles. Recent historians have described palace life at the time as something other than the picture of leisure amidst splendor painted by earlier generations of historians. One modern historian has called Versailles a "curious place: a mixture of work and play, splendor and filth, piety and licence."

GIRAUDON/ART RESOURCE

ish Succession came to an end.

The greatest winner was obviously Great Britain. Now a formidable commercial power in the Mediterranean, Latin America, and the North Atlantic, Britain was secure from French invasion and political meddling in its domestic affairs. However, France had been able to withstand the combined might of the Grand Alliance and to retain most of her American colonies and her 1678 frontiers in Europe, albeit at great human and financial cost.

7

Twilight

The troubles of the war brought Louis XIV a long series of adversities and sorrows. He had long made it his habit to keep the press under his control and to suppress public opinion when it displeased him. Louis's recklessness in both foreign and domestic policy—much of it inspired by Louvois—had made an irreversible impact on Europe. Such actions as the Reunions, the revocation of the Edict of Nantes, and the senseless destruction inflicted on the Palatinate had generated widespread, ever louder criticism. Accustomed to regarding himself as above criticism, Louis felt its sting. Now and again food riots broke out and had to be suppressed. During the harsh winter of 1709, he was forced to cut down hundreds of acres of forests to supply wood to the poor. For the first time ever in his reign, he appealed directly to the French people in this hour of need.

Louis XIV's great-grandson, Louis XV (1710–74), succeeded to the French throne upon the Sun King's death. Louis XV would eventually preside over a nation disfigured by inept government, disordered finances, and increasing popular hatred of the monarchy.

THE BETTMANN ARCHIVE

Louis's grandson Philip, who became King Philip V of Spain in 1700, was not to enjoy security in that position until 1713, when he was recognized as rightful monarch by Britain, the Dutch republic, Portugal, and Savoy.

GIRAUDON/ART RESOURCE

Louis visits the Gobelins workshops. The artifacts produced by the Gobelins came to adorn royal palaces throughout France and were also presented to foreign ambassadors to promote the glory of French artistry abroad.

An early 18th-century engraving portrays the terrible condition to which France had been reduced by the end of Louis's reign. Military spending had wrecked the economy, and successive bad harvests—combined with the collapse of the currency—had produced widespread poverty and famine.

To help raise money for the war effort, he sold many of his Versailles treasures. Dishes and tableware made of gold, along with silver furniture and candelabras, were melted down to replenish the court's depleted funds. He even pawned his crown jewels and begged for loans—an act the duke of Saint-Simon described as "the prostitution of the king." Merchants, no longer trusting the king's creditworthiness, demanded payment in cash, as they had done during the terrible armed rebellion of the Frondes.

He faced defeat and humiliation on the battlefield, political reverses at home, and, finally, catastrophe in his family. Louis was overwhelmed with grief. In April 1711 his son, the Great Dauphin, died of smallpox; less than a year later, stricken with measles his grandson, the duke of Burgundy, his wife, and their elder son, the duke of Brittany, died within a few weeks of each other in February and March 1712; another grandson, the duke of Berry, died in 1714. As a result, the only surviving direct heirs (not counting his illegitimate or recognized children by various mistresses) were his third grandson, Philip V of Spain, his nephew, Philip of Orléans, and his great-grandson, born in 1710, the future King Louis XV.

To ensure continuity and prevent a War of the French Succession, in case Philip V refused to abide by his Utrecht renunciation of the French throne, Louis wrote his testament on August 2, 1714, by which he named his nephew regent, adding that he must govern with the help of a Council of Trusteeship during young Louis's minority.

Tired and sick, Louis XIV suffered the last indignities of old age. Suffering from numerous stomach ailments (he had always been a compulsive and immoderate eater) and an advanced case of gangrene, he bore all without complaint or despair. After several days of painful attacks in August 1715, he prepared for death, leaving final instructions and advice to the four-and-a-half-year-old dauphin: "I have loved war too much, in this do not imitate me, nor in my all-too enormous expenditures." He died at 8:15 on the morning of Sunday, September 1, four days short of his 77th birthday. He had ruled France for 54 years.

He left behind a larger France with greater land claims in Europe and America than he had inherited from his father, although the wars to achieve these conquests reduced the country's financial resources to the verge of bankruptcy. Census figures estimated the population at between 17 and 20 million people, most of whom lived in poverty, even after

Archbishop François de Salignac de La Mothe Fénelon (1651–1715) is believed to have been the author of the letter—written in 1695 and addressed to Louis—that some scholars consider one of history's most powerful indictments of the king. "Your people are dying of hunger," it read. "All France is . . . one great poorhouse, desolate and unprovided."

Louis meets with Frederick Augustus I, elector of Saxony and (as Augustus II) king of Poland (1670–1733), in 1714. Relations between France and Saxony were erratic throughout Louis's reign: Frederick Augustus I's father, Elector John George III (1647–91) had been fiercely opposed to Louis, while his grandfather, Elector John George II (1613–80), had been a trusted ally and major recipient of French financial backing.

ART RESOURCE

the record harvests of 1714 and 1715. Expanded commerce and manufacturing begun under Louis's rule continued. During Louis's long reign, France excelled in the arts and letters, leaving intellectual and artistic accomplishments of enduring greatness. Due to almost constant military engagements and the treaty negotiations that resulted, French became the official diplomatic language for international negotiations. There already were currents of intellectual and religious dissension that questioned the divine right of kings, the relationship between governed and governors, and God's presence in the universe.

The reign of Louis XIV had been glorious in its aspirations but often destructive in its actions. Louis rebuilt the French economy through industrial modernization, increased trade, and colonial expansion, only to spend enormous sums outfitting France for war. His generals were kept constantly in battle to secure royal successions, punish opposition to the king's will, and always to make France the most powerful nation in Europe.

Louis ruthlessly persecuted those among his own people he considered heretics; he was capable of wanton violence against foreign populations. Ultimately these campaigns led to the Grand Alliance, with Europe united against France. The United Provinces, which Louis had unsuccessfully challenged, lost supremacy at sea, but now held more territory on land. In Spain, the French designate to the throne was unable to restore the weakened economy and ruined empire.

Seeing that the king was soon to die, his courtiers deserted him during his last days; after Louis asked Madame de Maintenon to leave his chambers, only a few servants remained at his bedside to witness his death. He asked them, as they wept, if they had thought he would live forever. From the age of five, Louis XIV had been king of France. That the king had ruled too long was an opinion commonly heard on the streets of Paris when news of his death reached the populace. Three-quarters of a century would pass before the absolute monarchy Louis established would be overthrown.

Philosopher René Descartes (1596–1650) was one of the many French thinkers who deserted his homeland in pursuit of the greater intellectual freedom that was generally to be found in Europe's Protestant kingdoms, republics, and principalities during the 17th century. The trend begun by Descartes and his fellow exiles had continued throughout Louis's reign.

Louis died at Versailles on September 1, 1715, of natural causes, at age 76. The mourning that was observed throughout the nation he had ruled for 61 years was strictly official; most of his long-suffering subjects felt immense relief at his passing. One commentator wrote that "the common people . . . openly returned thanks to God" upon learning of the Sun King's death.

Further Reading

Buranelli, Vincent. *Louis XIV.* Boston, Massachusetts: G. K. Hall & Co., 1966.

Erlanger, Philippe. *Louis XIV.* New York: Praeger Publishers, 1970.

Forster, Elborg, ed. *A Woman's Life in the Court of the Sun King.* Baltimore, Maryland: Johns Hopkins University Press, 1984.

Goubert, Pierre. *Louis XIV and Twenty Million Frenchmen.* New York: Random House, Inc., 1970.

Hilbert, Christopher. *Versailles.* New York: Newsweek Books, 1972.

Mitford, Nancy. *The Sun King.* New York: Harper & Row Publishers, Inc., 1966.

Ogg, David. *Louis XIV.* London: Oxford University Press, 1933.

Rothrug, Lionel. *Opposition to Louis XIV.* Princeton, New Jersey: Princeton University Press, 1965.

Scoville, Warren C. *The Persecution of the Huguenots and French Economic Development.* Berkeley, California: University of California Press, 1960.

Treasure, Geoffrey. *Seventeenth Century France.* New York: Barnes & Noble Books, 1966.

Chronology

Sept. 5, 1638	Born Louis XIV, the son of King Louis XIII of France and Anne of Austria, at the castle of Saint-Germain-en-Laye
May 14, 1643	Louis XIII dies Anne of Austria assumes power as regent for Louis XIV, with Jules Mazarin as her chief minister
1648	European powers sign the Peace of Westphalia, which ends the Thirty Years' War and gives most of Alsace to France
1648–53	Disgruntled Parlement members and nobles rebel against the French government in a series of uprisings known as the *Fronde*
Sept. 7, 1651	Louis XIV declares his majority
1659	Spain forced, by the Treaty of the Pyrenees, to cede to France much of Artois and all of Roussillon
June 9, 1660	Louis XIV weds Maria Theresa, the eldest daughter of the Spanish king, Philip IV
March 9, 1661	Louis XIV becomes undisputed ruler of France after Mazarin dies
1661	Consolidates power by arresting Nicolas Fouquet — the superintendent-general of finance — and refusing to appoint a chief minister Construction begins on Versailles, Louis's royal palace
1667–68	The War of Devolution: French troops capture part of the Spanish Netherlands, claimed by Louis XIV on the basis of marriage
1672	Dutch War begins when French troops occupy Holland Holland saved by the breaching of the dikes
1679	Louis's military success reaches its pinnacle as the Peace of Nijmegen is concluded, ending the Dutch War, and giving
1679–84	French courts called Chambers of Reunion convene to interpret recent treaties
1684	Louis XIV secretly marries Madame de Maintenon
Oct. 22, 1685	Revokes the Edict of Nantes, which had granted civil and religious liberties to French Protestants
1689–97	France fights the War of the League of Augsburg against England, Austria, Spain, Sweden, Holland and Bavaria
1697	Peace of Ryswick signed, forcing France to relinquish all territories acquired since 1667, except Strasbourg
1700	Louis XIV installs his grandson Philip as the king of Spain
1702–13	War of the Spanish Succession, ended by the Treaty of Utrecht and the Treaty of Rastadt
Sept. 1, 1715	Louis XIV dies, aged 77, at Versailles, of natural causes Louis XV, his great-grandson, becomes the new king of France under the regency of Philip, duke of Orléans

Index

Pierre L. Horn was born in Paris, France, where he studied at the Lycée Voltaire. He received his B.A. from Brooklyn College and his M.A. and Ph.D. from Columbia University. A member of the Wright State University faculty, Professor Horn has written extensively on French literature and culture. His works include a study of Marguerite Yourcenar, the first woman writer elected to the French Academy. Dr. Horn, who lives in Beavercreek, Ohio, was made a Chevalier dans L'Ordre des Palmes Academiques by the French government in 1978.

Arthur M. Schlesinger, jr., taught history at Harvard for many years and is currently Albert Schweitzer Professor of the Humanities at City University of New York. He is the author of numerous highly praised works in American history and has twice been awarded the Pulitzer Prize. He served in the White House as special assistant to Presidents Kennedy and Johnson.